Pastoral Ministry
according to PAUL

Pastoral Ministry according to PAUL

A Biblical Vision

James W. Thompson

Baker Academic
Grand Rapids, Michigan

Published by Baker Academic
a division of Baker Publishing Group
P.O. Box 6287, Grand Rapids, MI 49516-6287
www.bakeracademic.com

Printed in the United States of America

Library of Congress Cataloging-in-Publication Data
Thompson, James, 1942–
    Pastoral ministry according to Paul : a biblical vision / James W. Thompson.
        p.   cm.
    Includes bibliographical references and indexes.
    ISBN 0-8010-3109-5 (pbk.)
        1. Pastoral theology—Biblical teaching. 2. Paul, the Apostle, Saint.
    3. Bible. N.T. Epistles of Paul—Criticism, interpretation, etc. I. Title.
    BS2655.P3T48 2006
    253.09'015—dc22   2005027812

Contents

I

Discovering a Pauline
Pastoral Theology

After years of educating future ministers, my colleagues and I finally took on the task of writing a vision statement to serve as a foundation for our curriculum and to describe the ministry for which we were preparing our students. After I took the responsibility of chairing the committee and drafting the vision statement, I realized what a difficult task I had, offering a coherent vision that would reflect the faculty's shared understanding of the ministry. This challenge was especially remarkable in that faculty members could reach agreement on the final draft only after extended discussion even though we had been shaped in the same theological tradition and were preparing students for ministry within this tradition. We discovered that we work with many unstated and differing assumptions about the nature of the ministry.

When I talk to pulpit search committees who are prospective employers of our graduates, I discover that their vision of ministry scarcely corresponds to the vision that we hammered out as a faculty. These search committees present job descriptions with very specific expectations for ministerial candidates. Although these job descriptions do not articulate a theology of ministry, they reflect assumptions about the nature of the ministry. The assumptions derive primarily from the committees' own past experiences and observation of what appeared to be effective ministries.

From what I have learned from colleagues in other seminaries, my experience is not unique. Everyone has unstated assumptions about the nature of the ministry that are evident in the various alternative—even competing—models. Jackson Carroll has indicated that theological traditions have differing understandings of ministry. Denominations in the Reformed tradition emphasize a learned presentation of the faith whereas Methodists place great value on interpersonal skills. Southern Baptists emphasize evangelistic skills whereas Orthodox Christians expect liturgical leadership.[1] In the North American context, however, expectations have changed over a period of time, often crossing denominational lines.

My observation of developments within my own tradition correspond in large measure to the historical delineation described by John B. Cobb and Joseph Hough for developments in many denominations.[2] For an earlier generation, the ideal minister was the evangelist who was measured by his success in persuading large numbers of people to become Christians. Some were traveling revivalists, and countless others worked in local congregations where they were appointed primarily for evangelistic purposes. In a second era, congregational expectations for the minister shifted from outreach to nurturing the congregation and responding to the needs of individuals. In this era, ministers learned the techniques of the therapist and placed considerable value on pastoral care and counseling.

    1. Jackson W. Carroll, *As One with Authority* (Louisville: Westminster John Knox, 1991), 53. See also Donald E. Messer, *Contemporary Images of Ministry* (Nashville: Abingdon, 1989), 33–46.
    2. Joseph Hough and John B. Cobb Jr., *Christian Identity and Theological Education* (Atlanta: Scholars Press, 1985). I owe the reference to Carroll, *As One*, 53.

Their task was to meet the ever-increasing perceived needs of the people in the congregation. In the present era, the minister is ultimately measured by the ability to organize, build, and manage a complex organization. Congregations continue to assume that the minister will maintain the traditional roles of marrying and burying, but they believe that the ultimate goal of the minister is to take the congregation to a new level of growth. The minister must be both an effective communicator and an administrator. In a competitive religious marketplace, the task of the minister is to ensure that the congregation maintains its place among religious consumers. Often search committees no longer look for someone who conforms to one of these models. Instead they seek someone who is a combination of, for instance, Jay Leno, Lee Iacocca, and Dr. Phil.

These often unstated assumptions indicate that the missing dimension in the conversation about ministry is a theologically coherent understanding of the purpose of ministry that incorporates the numerous roles of the minister. According to Thomas Oden, "no systematic, scripturally grounded pastoral theology has been written for an English-speaking ecumenical audience since Washington Gladden's *The Christian Pastor* (1898)."[3] The literature on the various tasks of the minister is abundant, but we lack a comprehensive theological understanding that provides the foundation for the minister's many tasks.

We are searching for a unifying, centered view of ministry. Regrettably, the disciplines serving the modern pastoral office have become segmented into wandering, at times, prodigal, subspecializations. Although we have produced an abundance of literature on pastoral counseling, the question remains as to what is "pastoral" (*distinctively* pastoral) about so-called pastoral counseling. Sermons abound, and sermonic aids superabound, but few operate out of an integrated conception of the pastoral office that melds liturgical, catechetical, counseling, and equipping ministries. Having borrowed heavily from pragmatic management procedure while forgetting much of

3. Thomas Oden, *Pastoral Theology* (San Francisco: Harper and Row, 1983), 9.

their traditional rootage, church administration has become an orphan discipline vaguely wondering about its true parentage. The loss of a centered identity in ministry is mirrored in the excessive drive toward specialization of the disciplines intended to serve and unify ministry.[4]

The seminary curriculum does little to produce a coherent understanding of the telos of ministry. The division of the curriculum into separate areas of specialization, developed under the influence of the German model at the end of the nineteenth century, exacerbates the problem by separating ministry from the other theological disciplines.[5] Edward Farley has described the separation of the theological disciplines under the influence of German scholarship, indicating that contemporary theological schools have inherited the nineteenth-century understanding of the place of practical theology within a theological curriculum. Farley traces the development from the time when "practical theology" designated all theological study to the time when it became a separate discipline. In the initial step toward this separation, practical theology included moral theology, church polity, and other pastoral activities. As specialization increased, practical theology was distinguished from moral theology as an area pertaining to the church's fundamental activities.[6] The focus turned to the necessary skills for the maintenance of the church and the care of troubled people. Practical theology became segmented into a variety of subdisciplines. With this focus on the skills necessary for maintaining the church, seminaries and churches offered alternative, if not competing, definitions of pastoral care. Although the seminary degree requires both theory and praxis, the two areas are insufficiently related to each other to provide a theological foundation for ministry.

4. Ibid., 3.
5. David Kelsey, *Between Athens and Berlin* (Grand Rapids: Eerdmans, 1993), 63; Edward Farley, "Interpreting Situations: An Inquiry into the Nature of Practical Theology," in *Formation and Reflection*, ed. Lewis S. Mudge and James N. Poling (Philadelphia: Fortress, 1987), 2. See also Edward Farley, *Theologia: The Fragmentation and Unity of Theological Education* (Philadelphia: Fortress, 1983), 44.
6. Farley, *Theologia*, 44.

Without a theological foundation, the minister too easily becomes the one who ensures the church's competitive edge in the marketplace of consumer religion.

Despite the pressures that often come from the church and society to define the minister's role in pragmatic terms as the maintenance and growth of the institution, the answer to the question of ministerial identity, as Elle~ ̄ ̄ ̄ ;
a theological one.[7] In this book I a
sion in the conversation about ministr,   l
theology that rests on a conversation with recent interpreters of Pauline theology. Examining the theological foundations and goals of Paul's pastoral work, I argue that the Pauline vision will contribute to the discussion that now occupies churches and seminaries throughout North America: What is a minister? For what roles do we prepare future ministers? What are the goals of ministry? As a New Testament scholar who often works on the boundary between biblical studies and practical ministry, I wish to initiate a conversation between the two disciplines, for Paul provides a coherent pastoral vision that can be the basis for a contemporary pastoral theology. My purpose is to move beyond the focus on the roles of the minister and the how-to literature of ministry in order to determine the ultimate aims of our work. Others have challenged us to renew this theological dimension by returning to the classical texts concerning ministry.[8] Although engagement with the classical texts is a valuable exercise, I propose that we consider going beyond these ancient texts to a reconsideration of the significance of Pauline theology for defining the goals of ministry.

Paul is not the only guide for a pastoral theology, as several interpreters have shown. Eugene Peterson suggests that the Megilloth—Song of Solomon, Ruth, Lamentations, Ecclesiastes, and Lamentations—served an important pastoral purpose in ancient Israel, one that can be useful for shaping the imagination

7. Ellen Charry, *By the Renewing of Your Minds: The Pastoral Significance of Doctrine* (New York: Oxford University Press, 1997), vii.
8. See Andrew Purves, *Pastoral Care in the Classical Tradition* (Louisville: Westminster John Knox, 2001).

of the contemporary church.[9] Gustav Stählin affirms that "the New Testament is through and through a pastoral book," but he gives special emphasis to Matthew's narrative as an example of pastoral care.[10] Matthew shows pastoral concern for the situation of his readers; the combination of story and instruction gives joy and direction to a community in distress. Paul Walaskay finds the theological foundation for pastoral care in the healing traditions of the Old Testament and the Gospels.[11] Others look to the portraits of Jesus in the Gospels to identify a basic orientation for pastoral care.[12] Nevertheless, Paul's letters have a special value in delineating an understanding of the ultimate goal of ministry. The letters allow us to overhear Paul's pastoral guidance for his churches and to observe his pastoral theology in practice. They present a partial longitudinal study of Paul's role as evangelist, church planter, and pastor. Because such a comprehensive understanding of the goal of ministry is unparalleled among other biblical writers, Pauline theology constitutes an indispensable guide to us as we reflect on the ultimate goal of our ministry.

To engage Pauline and pastoral studies in conversation is to face methodological issues that arise from several factors. First, we lack a single definition of ministry or pastoral care as a basis for comparison with Paul. Second, neither Paul nor his coworkers functioned in a way parallel to the modern concept of the minister; ministry in our time is vastly different from anything in Jewish and Christian history or the New Testament.[13] And third, we face the hermeneutical challenge of appropriating

9. Eugene H. Peterson, *Five Smooth Stones for Pastoral Work* (Atlanta: John Knox, 1975), 21.

10. Gustav Stählin, "Von der Seelsorge im Neuen Testament," *Theologische Beiträge* 5 (1974): 105–17.

11. Paul W. Walaskay, "Biblical and Classical Foundations of the Healing Ministries," *Journal of Pastoral Care* 37 (1983): 195–206.

12. See Gottfried Schille, "Ist Seelsorge im Neuen Testament begründet?" *Die Zeichen der Zeit* 20 (1966): 128. Cf. Seward Hiltner, *The Christian Shepherd: Some Aspects of Pastoral Care* (New York: Abingdon, 1959), 22. See also Thomas Oden, *Kerygma and Counseling* (Philadelphia: Westminster, 1966), 154.

13. Don S. Browning, *The Moral Context of Pastoral Care* (Philadelphia: Westminster, 1976), 68.

Paul's ministry to the contemporary situation, for one cannot simply read a pastoral theology off the pages of the Bible without merging the horizons of the Bible's world and our own.[14] These problems indicate the methodological difficulty of discovering a Pauline theology of pastoral care. Still, I am convinced that we may find that insight into Paul provides a foundation for the contemporary church. Since it would be fruitless to begin with our own definitions of ministry and then examine the Pauline corpus to find a corollary, I suggest that we begin with a preliminary and general definition in which we see points of contact between our own understanding and that found in the Pauline Letters. One such point of contact is the recognition that Paul is the evangelist who not only initiates his converts into the faith but also has "anxiety for all of the churches" (2 Cor. 11:28). We may also observe functional similarities between our own understanding of the ministry and the activities of Paul in his concern for his converts.[15] Although emphases have varied through the centuries, certain elements have proved constant, including the offer of compassion, nurture, and comfort to others, especially members of the Christian community. Paul's work is sufficiently analogous to our own understanding of ministry for us to recognize in him a model for ministry, especially in the goals that he sets forth.

Pauline Pastoral Theology in Previous Study

I am not the first to suggest that Paul is the basis for a pastoral theology. Indeed, interpreters appeal to Paul's letters to support the alternative views of the goals of ministry mentioned above. For some, Paul is the basis for understanding the

14. William Challis, *The Word of Life: Using the Bible in Pastoral Care* (London: Marshall Pickering, 1997), 79.

15. See Kristlieb Adloff, "Paulus," in *Geschichte der Seelsorge in Einzelporträts*, vol. 1, *Von Hiob bis Thomas von Kempen* (Göttingen: Vandenhoeck und Ruprecht, 1994), 55–67. Adloff sees these points of contact in Paul's sympathy, comfort, and tenderness toward his listeners.

minister primarily as an evangelist; for others, Paul is the basis for understanding the minister as therapist. And according to recent literature on church growth, Paul provides the theological basis for the minister as a church planter and builder. Paul's statement "I planted, Apollos watered, but God gave the growth" (1 Cor. 3:6) is the foundation for a ministry focused on church growth. The mission of the church, according to this view, is to grow and extend God's reign through the planting and developing of churches.[16] Paul's metaphor of the building in 1 Corinthians 3:10–17 provides a further image of the minister as one who builds the congregation through effective planning and organization.

Although Paul employs the language of church growth in 1 Corinthians 3:6–9, he does not use the language in a way that supports the contemporary appeal to this Pauline passage. The context of the passage indicates that Paul's major concern is not with numerical growth but with the maturation of the church that he planted. In 1 Corinthians 3:1–5, Paul has used the imagery of infancy and maturity to describe the development of the church that he desires. The Corinthians, however, have not grown out of infancy, for they are engaged in the petty jealousy that characterized them before they became Christians. With their partisan politics—"I am of Paul, I am of Apollos"—they demonstrate that they are still in their infancy. The focus of Paul's imagery of planting and growth is that, despite the Corinthians' focus on individual leaders, "God gives the increase." In the images of planting, growth, and building, Paul's emphasis is on the maturing of the congregation. Although we may assume that Paul anticipates numerical

16. See Rick Warren, *The Purpose-Driven Church: Church Growth without Compromising Your Message* (Grand Rapids: Zondervan, 1995). See also Christian A. Schwarz, *Natural Church Development* (Carol Stream, IL: ChurchSmart Resources, 1966), 10: "We should not attempt to 'manufacture' church growth, but rather to release biotic potential which God has put into every church. It is our task to minimize obstacles to growth and multiplication within churches. Then church growth can happen 'all by itself.' God will do what he promised to do. He will grant growth." C. Peter Wagner, *Effective Body Building: Biblical Steps to Spiritual Growth* (San Bernardino, CA: Here's Life, 1982) uses 1 Corinthians as a textbook on church growth.

growth, his emphasis here is on growing up to maturity. He uses the building metaphor to ensure that the community's leaders build a community that will withstand the ultimate test. Earlier interpreters appealed to the Protestant focus on the Pauline doctrine of justification by faith, commonly understood as the center of his theology, to develop a pastoral theology. This understanding of justification by faith has contributed two dimensions to the traditional understanding of ministry. In the first place, the traditional view of justification by faith as the salvation of the individual has been the foundation for understanding the minister as the evangelist who offers God's grace to individuals and invites them to respond in faith. For those who understand justification by faith as a theology about "getting into" a relationship with God, ministry becomes the practice of getting people into God's grace through evangelism. Thus the role of the minister as evangelist corresponds to the traditional understanding of justification by faith.

In the second place, justification by faith has also been the basis for viewing ministry as the offer of grace to individuals who suffer from continuing conflicts in their attempt to live the Christian life. In the traditional interpretation of Romans 7, for example, the tormented person who says, "I do not do what I want, but I do the very thing I hate" (Rom. 7:15), is the Christian who is righteous and a sinner at the same time. Luther noted the pastoral significance of his interpretation when he said, "Indeed, it is a great consolation to us to learn that such a great apostle was involved in the same grievings and afflictions in which we find ourselves when we wish to be obedient to God!"[17] Since this person stands constantly in need of grace, the role of the minister is to communicate God's grace.

Howard Clinebell cites this passage as a basis for modern pastoral care. He speaks of Paul's "inner conflict" as an example of the human brokenness to which the minister responds: "All of us know the inner conflict expressed by Paul in his letter to the early Church in Rome: 'For even though the desire to

17. Martin Luther, *Lectures on Romans* (London: SCM, 1961), 208.

do good is in me, I am not able to do it. I don't do the good I want to do; instead, I do the evil that I do not want to do' (Rom. 7:18–19, GNB)."[18] For Clinebell, this passage illustrates that "our estrangement from ourselves and others is somehow rooted in our estrangement from God's life-giving love."[19] This estrangement provides the basis for pastoral care, defining the role of the pastor as one who responds to troubled persons, helping them overcome this estrangement.

We may see the impact of this understanding of justification in the work of pastoral theologians who equate the doctrine of justification by faith with the acceptance that stood at the center of Rogerian psychotherapy. Clinebell appeals to Paul when he describes the counseling relationship as "a channel for the grace of God, the transforming love that is the source of all salvation and all wholeness (Gal. 2:8; Rom. 3:23–41)."[20] According to LeRoy Aden, "Paul never lets us forget that God accepts us in spite of our being unacceptable, that he loves and forgives even though we continue to show enmity and disbelief toward him. Out of this unconditional, undeserved acceptance flows a love that seeks to serve even as it has been served."[21] We may compare this comment from Rodney Hunter:

> From the perspective of Paul and the Protestant Reformers, the heart of the Gospel, from which all else in Christian faith, life, and ministry flows, is the message that God has forgiven our sin, that he has not held our trespasses against us, but by the free giving of his Son has proclaimed and established our reconciliation with Him in faith, totally apart from all considerations of merit or deserving. In this tradition, the heart of the Gospel is the announcement of the forgiveness of sins through Jesus Christ. . . .

18. Howard Clinebell, *Basic Types of Pastoral Care and Counseling: Resources for the Ministry of Healing and Growth*, rev. ed. (Nashville: Abingdon, 1984), 58.
19. Ibid.
20. Ibid., 55.
21. LeRoy Aden, "Pastoral Care and the Gospel," in *The Church and Pastoral Care*, ed. LeRoy Aden and J. Harold Ellens (Grand Rapids: Baker, 1988), 34.

If this message is taken as the central theme of the Christian faith—as it has been traditionally in Protestant faith and theology—then it must also comprise the central or focal theme for ministry, including the ministry of pastoral care. Within this context, from a purely normative and systematic standpoint, pastoral care as well as the more specialized ministries of counseling are to be understood, fundamentally and comprehensively, with reference to this theme.[22]

Paul's doctrine of grace becomes the basis for a pastoral understanding of acceptance.

Although Paul has sometimes been used as a source of pastoral theology, this common use is based on an antiquated and inadequate understanding of Paul. In the first place, it rests on an assumption highly debatable in biblical scholarship: that justification is the center of Paul's theology and that it consists of forgiveness for the individual. With its individualized focus, it does not acknowledge that justification includes not only getting into a relationship with God through forgiveness but God's covenant faithfulness, which both accepts sinners and reclaims them for a new existence.[23] Furthermore, it does not acknowledge the polemical context in which Paul formulated the doctrine of justification in Galatians and Romans. Thus a pastoral theology based on a traditional understanding of Paul's doctrine of justification by faith engages neither the full ramifications of justification nor other aspects of Paul's theology. In the second place, it ignores the corporate nature of Christian existence, offering an individualized understanding of justification by faith. Finally, it ignores Paul's consistent call for trans-

22. Rodney Hunter, "Law and Gospel in Pastoral Care," *Journal of Pastoral Care* 30 (1976): 146.
23. See Gerald L. Borchert, "Romans, Pastoral Counseling, and the Introspective Conscience of the West," *Review and Expositor* 83 (1986): 83, for additional problems with the Protestant emphasis on "getting in": "It is my impression that a major weakness in discussions of Romans is that Western church leaders since Luther have, for the most part, been limited in their analyses of Paul's view of salvation. This limitation is a direct result of Protestantism's overemphasis upon justification and the failure to reckon with the movement in Paul's thinking from justification through to other aspects of the salvation process."

formation and his paraenetic instructions, according to which he insists that Christians walk "worthily of the gospel."

If Paul is to provide a theological foundation for pastoral care, we must see a more nuanced understanding of his theology. Therefore, since all theology has a pastoral dimension for Paul, we cannot assume that justification by faith, narrowly defined as God's acceptance of the individual, provides the basis for a pastoral theology, for Paul's concerns extend beyond merely getting into a relationship with God. If we look at the range of Paul's letters, we see that justification has a central place only in Galatians and Romans. Paul appeals to this theme only in polemical contexts to declare who belongs among the covenant people. Its focus is not on the individual who struggles to find a gracious God but on God's faithfulness to the covenant with Israel, which now includes the Gentiles. This understanding has consequences for traditional views of ministry, for it focuses more on ecclesiology than on the individual's response to the gospel. Consequently, although justification is an important theme in Paul's theology, it is not the center of his thought. Moreover, as argued below, although Paul's theology provides a warrant for evangelism, the telos of his work extends beyond bringing sinners into a relationship with God to the complete formation of his communities.

Krister Stendahl challenged the common Western interpretation of Romans 7, arguing that Paul gives no evidence that he struggled with sin either before or after his conversion.[24] Interpreters in the last generation have argued that the passage speaks neither of Paul's pre-Christian experience nor of his Christian life but of Paul's new Christian perspective on the individual under law. Thus if Romans 7 does not describe the Christian's need for grace and acceptance, it does not function as the basis for the theology of acceptance that has provided the foundation for pastoral theology.

24. Krister Stendahl, "Paul and the Introspective Conscience of the West," *Harvard Theological Review* 56 (1963): 200–202.

An additional weakness of the traditional understanding of justification is that it diminishes the importance of ethics, separating pastoral theology from ethical transformation. Although Paul's writings insist that justification does not undermine ethics (cf. Rom. 6:1–11), interpreters have relegated ethical change to the margins of Pauline theology, turning Paul's doctrine of grace into "cheap grace." Consequently, pastoral theology has created a wide gulf between acceptance of the individual and the demand for the obedience of faith.[25]

A New Perspective on Paul for Pastoral Theology

Although numerous studies have explored the pastoral practices of Paul, the missing dimension in the study of Paul and ministry is the analysis of the ultimate goal of his pastoral work. Since justification by faith, conceived as individual salvation, is not the organizing principle for a pastoral theology, I shall offer an alternative. My task is not to offer a thorough Pauline theology but to show the correspondence between central theological themes and his pastoral goal. In the absence of a pastoral theology based on the traditional understanding of Paul, I suggest that a new reading of Paul provides the adequate foundation for a Pauline pastoral theology and offers a coherent vision of the aims of ministry. The center of Paul's thought is a theology of transformation, which provides the basis for Paul's pastoral theology.

A very consistent understanding of ministry emerges in all of the letters, allowing us to define it in precise terms: *ministry*

25. Douglas Harnick, *Paul among the Postliberals* (Grand Rapids: Brazos, 2003), 57. Note also p. 25: "When Protestants think of Paul, they think of the doctrine of justification by faith in Jesus Christ. Justification means being made right before God through faith alone in Jesus' atoning sacrifice alone, apart from the law or any other human workings or striving. That is the essence or core or peculiar contribution of Paul's theology." Cf. Oden, *Pastoral Theology*, 8: "Antinomianism is the weird, wild, impulsive, unpredictable sleeping partner of much contemporary pastoral care. It mistakes the gospel for license, freedom for unchecked self-actualization, and health for native vitalism."

*is participation in God's work of transforming the community
of faith until it is "blameless" at the coming of Christ.* The
community is unfinished business, standing between its beginning at baptism and its completion at the end. Paul's pastoral
ambition, as he states consistently in his letters, is community
formation. His Gentile communities now participate in Israel's
story, living between their initial adoption (or "election") into
that story and the final day, when they will be transformed
into the image of Jesus Christ. Paul's pastoral ambition is to
participate with God in effecting the transformation of his
communities.

J. Christiaan Beker has argued persuasively that an understanding of Paul's theology requires our recognition of both
the coherence and the contingency of Paul's letters.[26] We find
this coherence in the themes that Paul enunciates under a
variety of circumstances. I suggest that a pastoral theology
of transformation emerges as the center of Paul's thought
when one considers the following: (1) Paul offers a consistent
statement of his pastoral ambition in almost all of his letters.
(2) Paul's statements about his pastoral ambition are consistent
with the major themes in his theology. (3) Despite the variety
of circumstances in which Paul writes, his argument moves
toward ethical exhortation in his hope of shaping the church's
transformation.

Paul's Pastoral Ambition

A consistent feature of Paul's letters is the statement of his
pastoral vision, indicating the goal of his ministry. The per-
vasiveness of this ministerial vision in his letters reflects its
coherence within Pauline theology:

> Nevertheless on some points I have written to you rather boldly
> by way of reminder, because of the grace given me by God to be
> a minister of Christ Jesus to the Gentiles in the priestly service

26. J. Christiaan Beker, *Paul the Apostle: The Triumph of God in Life and Thought*
(Philadelphia: Fortress, 1980), 23–36.

of the gospel of God, so that the offering of the Gentiles may be acceptable, sanctified by the Holy Spirit. *In Christ Jesus, then, I have reason to boast of my work for God.* (Rom. 15:15–17)

According to the grace of God given to me, like a skilled master builder I laid a foundation, and someone else is building on it. Each builder must choose with care how to build on it. For no one can lay any foundation other than the one that has been laid; that foundation is Jesus Christ. Now if anyone builds on the foundation with gold, silver, precious stones, wood, hay, straw—the work of each builder will become visible, for the Day will disclose it, because it will be revealed with fire, and the fire will test what sort of work each has done. If what has been built on the foundation survives, the builder will receive a reward. If the work is burned up, the builder will suffer loss; the builder will be saved, but only as through fire. (1 Cor. 3:10–15)

Indeed, this is our boast, the testimony of our conscience: we have behaved in the world with frankness and godly sincerity, not by earthly wisdom but by the grace of God—and all the more toward you. For we write you nothing other than what you can read and also understand; I hope you will understand until the end—*as you have already understood us in part—that on the day of the Lord Jesus we are your boast even as you are our boast.* (2 Cor. 1:12–14)

I wish you would bear with me in a little foolishness. Do bear with me! I feel a divine jealousy for you, for I promised you in marriage to one husband, to present you as a chaste virgin to Christ. (2 Cor. 11:1–3)

Then I laid before them (though only in a private meeting with the acknowledged leaders) the gospel that I proclaim among the Gentiles, in order to make sure that I was not running, or had not run, in vain. (Gal. 2:2; cf. 4:11)

It is by your holding fast to the word of life that I can boast on the day of Christ that I did not run in vain or labor in vain. But even if I am being poured out as a libation over the sacrifice and the offering of your faith, I am glad and rejoice with all of

you—and in the same way you also must be glad and rejoice
with me. (Phil. 2:16–18)

*For what is our hope or joy or crown of boasting before our
Lord Jesus at his coming? Is it not you? Yes, you are our glory
and joy!* (1 Thess. 2:19–20)

In every instance in which Paul declares his pastoral ambition, he indicates that the success or failure of his work will
be determined only at the end, when he will either "boast"
of his work or realize that his work has been in vain.[27] The
eschatological horizon is a central feature of Paul's pastoral
ambition. Using language taken from Israel's story, he refers
consistently to the "day" (1 Cor. 3:13; 2 Cor. 1:14; Phil. 2:16)
that will reveal the quality of his work. He will "boast" of
work that has been accomplished (Rom. 15:17; 2 Cor. 1:14;
Phil. 2:16; 1 Thess. 2:19). A church that is "blameless" (Phil.
2:15–16) at the coming of Christ will be the goal of his work.
In the meantime, Paul indicates on some occasions that he is
already proud of his churches (cf. 2 Cor. 7:14; 8:24; 9:2) and of
the work that he has done on their behalf (1 Cor. 9:15), but on
other occasions he considers the prospect of working "in vain"
(Gal. 2:2; 4:11). His pastoral ambition is therefore corporate
and eschatological. Because the ultimate test of his ministry is
the outcome of his work with the churches, the ultimate goal
defines his ministry in the present.

Paul does not use the term "pastor" to describe his work;
instead he employs a variety of images to describe the eschatological and corporate goal of his work. He is the priest offering
the Gentiles as a sacrifice (Rom. 15:15–17), the builder whose
work will finally be tested (1 Cor. 3:10–17), the father of the
bride (2 Cor. 11:3) preparing for the wedding of his daughter,
the pregnant woman in travail before childbirth (Gal. 4:19),

---

27. See C. Spicq, *Theological Lexicon of the New Testament*, 3 vols. (Peabody,
MA: Hendrickson, 1994), 2:301. Paul normally uses the term *kauchēma* ("boast") in
a positive sense for what he is proud of—e.g., work that has been accomplished.

the sacrificial offering for the people (Phil. 2:16), and the father who is devoted to his children.

As an evangelist, Paul has brought his Gentile churches into this unfinished narrative. In his letters Paul regularly recalls the community's origins (Rom. 6:1–11; 1 Cor. 1:18–2:5; Gal. 3:1–6; Phil. 1:6, 11; 1 Thess. 1:5–10) and points toward its destination in God's grand narrative. In the meantime, he writes to ensure that the narrative comes to an appropriate conclusion. Paul assumes in his letters that, as a result of his original evangelistic mission, the converts experienced a radical change through the power of God. This change was only the beginning of the story (Phil. 1:6), which will come to an end on the day of Jesus Christ (Phil. 1:6, 11). Paul's pastoral care consists of his own participation in the work that God is doing in the transformation of his converts. Thus the letters speak not only of the new existence already attained but of the transformation that is occurring. The language of formation (*morph-*), always in the passive voice (Rom. 12:2; 2 Cor. 3:18; Gal. 4:19; Phil. 3:10, 21), indicates the central role of this concept in Pauline theology. Paul's pastoral theology is determined not only by God's acceptance of the ungodly but by God's formation of the people into the image of Christ. Paul thus articulates clearly that the goal of his work is to participate in the formation of the community.

The Shape of Paul's Letters

Paul's correspondence reveals his pastoral concern as he writes to nurture his converts. We discover this pastoral theology implicitly inasmuch as a constant element of his letters is the movement from theological reflection to the challenge Paul gives his churches to live "worthily of the gospel" (Phil. 1:27; cf. 1 Thess. 2:12). The consistency of the exhortations within the letters reflects Paul's pastoral theology, which is rooted in his expectation of moral progress among his readers. His pastoral theology is also implicit in the prayers at the beginning of the letters (cf. 1 Cor. 1:4–9; Phil. 1:3–11) inasmuch as they frequently describe Paul's hope for the ultimate outcome of his work. His initial evangelistic work is therefore only the beginning of a process that will not be complete until the end of time. His work will be successful only if his congregations live out the consequences of the gospel through transformed lives and are fully transformed at the coming of Christ. Thus all theology is pastoral for Paul. He and his communities share a narrative that begins with their conversion and will end when God will bring them to completion (Phil. 1:6), and the letters are written at the midpoint of the narrative.[28] His regular employment of the language of formation (*morph-*) to describe the progress of his communities (cf. Rom. 12:2; 2 Cor. 3:18; Gal. 4:19; Phil. 3:19–20) corresponds to the shape of his letters, for Paul's ethical advice reflects his pastoral ambition of participation in the ethical transformation of his communities. In his deep involvement with his converts, we find Paul's pastoral work.

Paul's Pastoral Vision and Theology

Paul's description of a communal narrative presupposes a larger narrative, according to which the God of the Old Testament has demonstrated covenant fidelity in Jesus Christ at the turn of the ages and will ultimately bring this narrative to an end. Inasmuch as Paul either alludes to or implies this narrative in all of his letters, it forms the substructure of his thought.[29] This narrative, stated simply, consists of the work of God with its beginning, middle, and end. At the beginning is God's creation, followed by human rebellion (cf. Rom. 5:12–21). Along

28. On the communal narrative of Paul's churches, see Bruce W. Longenecker, "Narrative Interest in the Study of Paul," in *Narrative Dynamics in Paul: A Critical Assessment*, ed. Bruce W. Longenecker (Louisville: Westminster John Knox, 2002), 13. See also Andrew T. Lincoln, "The Stories of Predecessors and Inheritors in Galatians and Romans," ibid., 175, where he says of these two letters, "The issue is whether they will be prepared to reconfigure their story in the light of the overarching story of the gospel on which Paul's attempt to persuade them draws."

29. See N. T. Wright, *The New Testament and the People of God* (Minneapolis: Fortress, 1992), 405.

the way, God calls Abraham and sets in motion Israel's story, which includes exile and restoration. The coming of Christ is the decisive act of God and the dominant "short story" that constitutes the turning point of the ages. The story will come to an end on the day of Christ. In the meantime Paul and his communities live between the middle and end of the story. The community of Gentiles has been adopted into Israel's story and now waits for the ultimate consummation of God's promises on the day of the Lord. Its conversion was an act of creation and election. Now the community awaits the ultimate day of the Lord. At the end, the community will be transformed into the image of God, regaining the primordial condition.

The recent literature on Paul has demonstrated that this narrative forms the substructure of Paul's reflection. Thus the doctrine of justification by faith is an essential element in this narrative: Paul employs this theme to declare God's final vindication of those who are within the covenant, and he announces that God has already "justified" those who now live within the covenant of faith. Paul's doctrine of sanctification also fits within this narrative framework, for he describes the moral progress that his converts make not only as transformation but also as sanctification (cf. 1 Thess. 3:11–13), and he envisions that his converts will be wholly sanctified at the final stage of the narrative (1 Thess. 5:23).

Paul's reflections begin with the transformation of Christ, the decisive turning point in the narrative. Morna Hooker has described this transformation as an "interchange" in which Christ "became what we are in order that we might become what he is."[30] Although the language comes from Irenaeus (*Adversus haereses* 5, praefatio), it accurately describes the consistent theme of Paul's letters. In the Christ event, Christ "became what we are." The ultimate goal is that humanity

---

30. Morna Hooker, "Interchange in Christ and Ethics," *Journal for the Study of the New Testament* 25 (1985): 5. Hooker explains that the metaphor comes from the "interchange" of roads at a busy intersection. When the car breaks down and is towed in a new direction, interchange occurs. This provides the metaphor for the Christ event, in which Christ comes to lead humans in a new direction.

be transformed into his image, that is, become "what he is."
Paul expresses this theme of interchange most clearly in the
following passages:

> For our sake he made him to be sin who knew no sin, so that
> in him we might become the righteousness of God. (2 Cor.
> 5:21 NRSV)

> For you know the generous act of our Lord Jesus Christ, that
> though he was rich, yet for your sakes he became poor, so that
> by his poverty you might become rich. (2 Cor. 8:9 NRSV)

> Christ redeemed us from the curse of the law by becoming a
> curse for us . . . in order that in Christ Jesus the blessing of
> Abraham might come to the Gentiles. (Gal. 3:13–14 NRSV)

> God sent his Son, born of a woman, born under the law, in
> order to redeem those who were under the law, so that we might
> receive adoption as children. (Gal. 4:4–5 NRSV)

> For God has done what the law, weakened by the flesh, could
> not do: by sending his own Son in the likeness of sinful flesh,
> and to deal with sin, he condemned sin in the flesh, so that
> the just requirement of the law might be fulfilled in us. (Rom.
> 8:3–4 NRSV)

These passages have a common structure. Paul describes
an event when Christ became something less than his original
status, participating in the weakness of human existence (i.e.,
he became "sin," "poor," the "curse"). This declaration is
followed by a purpose clause indicating what the believers
may become (i.e., "righteousness," "rich") or receive (a new
existence).[31] Thus the ultimate result of the Christ event is that
believers share in what Christ is. Those who are transformed by
Christ's sacrifice for others abandon their self-seeking in order

31. Morna D. Hooker, "A Partner in the Gospel: Paul's Understanding of His
Ministry," in *Theology and Ethics in Paul and His Interpreters*, ed. Eugene H. Lovering
Jr. and Jerry Sumney (Nashville: Abingdon, 1996), 90.

to live a new moral existence. They will finally be transformed into the image of the exalted one.

Although this formula of interchange does not appear in all of the letters, the theme is present. The letters, written under a variety of circumstances, reflect the dimensions of Paul's pastoral theology of transformation. In Philippians and 1 Thessalonians, Paul articulates his pastoral theology through his prayers and exhortations, speaking confidently of the communities' transformation and God's work in bringing them to completion on the day of Christ. God empowers the community "to will and to do" (Phil. 2:13) the good. Chapter 2 of this study examines Paul's theology of Christian formation and his role in this process.

Chapter 3 observes the complicating features of Paul's pastoral theology. According to Galatians 5:17, the progress of the community is not self-evident; Paul refers to the struggle between willing and doing. Despite the community's good beginning, the successful completion of the community's narrative is in doubt. Unlike the Philippians, in whom God "began a good work" (Phil. 1:6), the Galatians have "begun" in the Spirit, only to relapse to the flesh (Gal. 3:3). Paul's examination of the human difficulties and tensions that prevent the completion of the narrative come into view as Paul still holds out the hope that Christ will be formed among the Galatians (Gal. 4:19).

In Romans Paul expands on the issues of Galatians, again describing the struggle between willing and doing (Rom. 7:14–25) and holding out the promise of the ultimate transformation of the community of faith (Rom. 8:29; 12:2). The communal narrative includes the entrance into God's grand narrative at its beginning (Rom. 6:1–11) and the conclusion of the grand narrative. In the meantime, Paul challenges the community to "be transformed" in anticipation of the ultimate transformation. Chapter 4 of this study demonstrates the connection between Paul's theology of transformation and the goals of pastoral ministry.

In the Corinthian correspondence, Paul describes his work as the founder of the community with the metaphors of "planting"

and "building" (1 Cor. 3:6–17). With an alternative vision of
a building that remains under construction until the end (cf.
1 Cor. 3:10–17), Paul in both letters confronts readers who have
applied the cultural standards of Corinth to their understanding
of leadership. The task of the Christian leader is to work with
God in the construction of a building that will be complete
only at the end. Chapter 5 of this study analyzes the pastoral
theology of the Corinthian correspondence, indicating that a
community transformed by the cross is Paul's ultimate aim.

Paul's letters presuppose a narrative of the community's existence and a vision of wholeness. A constant feature in Paul's
letters is the emphasis on the wholeness of his communities.
His pastoral work is to ensure that the communities are transformed into the image of Christ. Thus transformation is a focal
point of Paul's pastoral theology. Chapter 6 indicates the constant features of Pauline theology that provide the theological
foundations for pastoral care and reflects on the hermeneutical
implications of our appeal to Paul.

Although my argument is drawn exclusively from the undisputed letters of Paul, the other letters also presuppose the same
corporate narrative as the basis for ministry. In both Colossians
and Ephesians, the church lives in the interim between Christ's
saving deed and the completion of God's work. It is "being renewed in knowledge according to the image of its creator" (Col.
3:10; cf. Eph. 4:24) and manifests God's transforming power as
it overcomes self-seeking and ethnic pride in order to be united in
the bond of peace (cf. Eph. 4:3). In Philemon, Paul writes to one
of his converts (Philemon) about another (Onesimus), guiding
Philemon to understand the communal implications of conversion and to receive his slave "as a beloved brother" (16). The
Pastoral Epistles presuppose a communal narrative in which the
outcome of Paul's work is threatened by heresy. In these letters,
as in the undisputed letters of Paul, the task of the minister is to
ensure the fidelity of the community from its founding until the
end. Paul's theology of transformation is evident in the ethical
guidance that he gives to all of his converts.

Paul's Pastoral Theology and the Contemporary Church

The historical distance between Paul and the contemporary church, as acknowledged above, demands that we exercise caution when we employ Paul's pastoral theology in our own time. As the founder of churches in a pagan environment, Paul could speak about a corporate narrative that is unknown to most contemporary congregations. Paul's task was to shape first-generation converts into a community that had experienced a new beginning; whereas, we minister primarily to communities in a Christian culture who have little sense of the radical break that creates a corporate memory. In our mobile society, our churches have little sense of a corporate narrative. Nevertheless, I am convinced that we can merge the horizons between the ministry of Paul and that of the contemporary minister. Paul's clear articulation of his pastoral ambition provides focus to the contemporary minister who struggles with a variety of expectations. His focus on community transformation is a welcome alternative to our own focus on meeting the individual needs of members of the congregation. Moreover, his call for a communal and countercultural ethic provides a missing dimension in the contemporary understanding of ministry. For Paul, all of the functions and skills of the minister fit within a pastoral theology of transformation.

Paul's ministry has a pastoral ambition that is transparent in all of his letters. As we shall see in the chapters that follow, this ministry does not always conform to the expectations of his churches. In some of them, the pastoral goals are gravely threatened; the transformation of his communities is in doubt. He never mentions the numerical growth of his churches. Nevertheless, he offers a coherent and unwavering view of his purpose as a minister. A careful analysis of his letters will provide the missing dimension in the contemporary conversation about the purpose of ministry.

2

Blameless at His Coming

Paul's Pastoral Vision in Philippians and 1 Thessalonians

Because the letters are substitutes for his presence, they present an important window into Paul's understanding of his ministry. Not only does Paul conduct his pastoral work through the medium of the letters; he also uses them to communicate his pastoral vision, especially transparent in Philippians and 1 Thessalonians. We begin with these letters because both are deeply pastoral letters written by the absent mentor to his new congregation, and the two share similarities of situation, purpose, and location. Despite scholarly attempts to find a doctrinal issue setting the agenda, little in these letters suggests that Paul writes with a dominant doctrinal issue at hand (see below). Rather, his concern in both letters is the future of the community: whether he has run in vain (Phil. 2:16; 1 Thess. 3:5). In contrast to Paul's other letters (e.g., 2 Corinthians, Galatians), in which he engages in impassioned polemic, here he expresses confidence in the progress of his communities.

With their focus on the moral progress of the readers, both letters resemble the ancient hortatory letter of friendship, in which the mentor writes to guide the reader in moral improvement.[1] The consistent theme of presence/absence demonstrates Paul's concern over the fate of the community. Here, through his prayers and exhortations, we see the pastoral vision for the church and his role in it.

The Pastoral Situation of the Letters

Despite the numerous attempts to identify the issues behind Philippians and 1 Thessalonians, we find only scattered direct references to the situation of these churches. In Philippians, Paul speaks of opposition only at 1:15–17; 3:2, 18–19. Because references to the false teachers are only glancing blows that function as a foil to sharpen the contrast between Paul's message and alternative modes of existence, we need not conclude that they are the major concern. Thus Paul spends no time arguing the issues raised in 3:2, 18–19, as he did in his more combative letters. The issue that he raises is the impact of his absence on the Philippians and the uncertainty raised by his recent imprisonment (1:12). Paul's statement that "it has been granted to us to suffer" (1:29) suggests that the Philippians also suffer for their faith. The dual emphases on joy and unity may suggest that, in the presence of uncertainty, the congregation suffers from fear and that fears from without have increased the tensions within the community.

In 1 Thessalonians, Paul says little about the situation. The readers had originally received the word of God "in spite of persecution" (1:6). Having abruptly left the Thessalonians, Paul had dispatched Timothy to encourage the Thessalonians "not

1. See Abraham J. Malherbe, *Paul and the Thessalonians* (Philadelphia: Fortress, 1987), 68–78; *The Letters to the Thessalonians,* Anchor Bible 32B (New York: Doubleday, 2000), 78–81; Stanley Stowers, "Friends and Enemies in the Politics of Heaven," in *Pauline Theology,* ed. Jouette M. Bassler, David M. Hay, and E. Elizabeth Johnson, 4 vols. (Minneapolis: Fortress, 1991–1997), 1:107–14.

to be shaken by tribulations" (3:3), which Paul has assured the Thessalonians would be their lot. Paul expresses gratitude that the Thessalonians have suffered the same things as their compatriots in Judea (2:14). In the immediate context, Timothy has brought a good report about the congregation (3:6). Thus we may assume that the Thessalonians have suffered the crisis of being faithful in a hostile climate.

From the references to the church's struggle with its environment, we may extrapolate more information about the probable situation of the Macedonian churches. We need not conclude that each of the issues mentioned in the two epistles reflects a local problem, for Paul writes not only to correct his readers but also to reinforce what they already know (cf. 1 Thess. 4:1–2). Nor must we read the issues of Galatians into Paul's references to opponents in Philippians 3:2. References to opposition from within the church may point to potential rather than real local concerns within Paul's churches.[2] Although the issues faced in Philippi and Thessalonica were probably not identical, in both instances Paul's absence has resulted in his concern for the churches and the mutual desire of Paul and the churches to see each other. In each instance, Paul has formed a community that would have been extraordinary in antiquity—one composed of people from diverse ethnic and social backgrounds. The continued viability of such a community was an obvious concern. Paul's challenge to "stand firm" against opponents who are on their way to destruction (Phil. 1:28), his reference to suffering for Christ, and his invitation to join him in the "struggle" (agōn) suggest that the church is confronted by threatening forces (Phil. 1:30). The Thessalonians recall that Paul first preached to them "in spite of great opposition" (1 Thess. 2:2) and that they experienced opposition from the beginning (1:6). Indeed, they followed their fellow Christians in

2. Stowers, "Friends and Enemies," 115–16. According to Stowers (p. 116), "a common mistranslation of *blepete* as 'beware' (3:2) makes the section appear less hortatory than it actually is. . . . When a direct object follows, *blepete* means 'consider' or 'reflect upon.'" Hence Paul is actually calling for the Philippians to reflect on negative examples that contrast with the behavior Paul encourages.

Judea in suffering (2:14). Paul's concern for the Thessalonians' response to distress has led him to send Timothy to ensure that the community has not been overcome by the persecutions (1 Thess. 3:2). Conversion inevitably created tensions within the families of Paul's new members and a negative reaction from their neighbors, resulting in a strong demarcation between "insiders" and "outsiders" (cf. Phil. 2:15–16; 1 Thess. 4:12).[3] Thus the persecutions were not systematic but probably consisted of discrimination, harassment, and social ostracism.[4] The continued loyalty of the church members to the community of faith was constantly being tested. These challenges are exacerbated by Paul's absence. In both letters Paul writes as a pastor who addresses the concrete circumstances of the Macedonian churches to encourage the community to maintain its faithfulness in his absence, despite the tensions from the surrounding environment. As a pastor, he presents a vision of what he wants his communities to become.

Paul's Pastoral Communication in Philippians

As with any hortatory letter of friendship, one occasion for correspondence can be the absence of the mentor from his pupil(s). But although Philippians refers to the theme of presence/absence several times (cf. 1:27, 24–25; 2:13), the letter reflects more than the theme of the absence of the mentor. Paul's imprisonment is the immediate occasion for this letter. Paul's repeated assurances to the Philippians (cf. 1:12, 24–25) suggest that his imprisonment has raised questions among the readers about the viability of their Christian commitment. The

3. See the discussion in Karl O. Sandnes, *A New Family: Conversion and Ecclesiology in the Early Church with Cross-cultural Comparisons* (Bern: Peter Lang, 1994), 21–31. Sandnes describes conversion as an offense against family honor in ancient cultures. See Malherbe, *Paul and the Thessalonians*, 36–46, for the crisis experienced by new converts to philosophy who had to abandon their usual relationships.
4. Malherbe, *Letters to the Thessalonians*, 172–73; *Paul and the Thessalonians*, 46–47; T. Holtz, *Der erste Brief an die Thessalonicher*, 3rd ed., Evangelisch-katholischer Kommentar zum Neuen Testament 13 (Zurich: Benziger, 1998), 13.

words of 1:12 indicate that a major purpose of the letter is to reassure the community that Paul's imprisonment does not mean the end of their new existence and to encourage the listeners to continue in their new Christian commitment. As the community faces the inevitable hostility of its neighbors (cf. 1:28), Paul writes to reassure and to challenge the Philippians to live in a way that is appropriate to the gospel whether he is present or absent (1:27). His reflections about the nature of the gospel thus provide the foundation for his ethical instructions.

Although scholars have frequently pointed to the breaks in Paul's argument in 3:1 and 4:10 as evidence that the letter is a composite of separate fragments, recent studies have shown that the letter contains a coherent argument for a change in the Philippians' attitudes within the community.[5] Paul's emphasis on future behavior corresponds to deliberative speech.[6] The opening salutation and thanksgiving (1:1–11) functions as the introduction (*exordium*),[7] in which Paul introduces his pastoral vision before he develops the theme in the remainder of the letter. His recollection of recent events and his reflection on his own state of mind (1:12–26) form the narrative (*narratio*), in which he lays the foundation for the argument that follows.[8] In 1:27–30 Paul states the case to be argued (*propositio*) in the letter: the call for harmony within the church. He develops the argument in 2:1–4:3 (the *probatio*) before reiterating it in 4:4–20 (the *peroratio*).[9]

5. See the discussion about separate fragments in Peter Wick, *Der Philipperbrief: Der formale Aufbau des Briefs als Schlüssel zum Verständnis seines Inhalts*, Beiträge zur Wissenschaft vom Neuen Testament (Stuttgart: Kohlhammer, 1993), 16–38.

6. Deliberative rhetoric commends or advises concerning a course of action for the future. See David E. Aune, *The Westminster Dictionary of New Testament and Early Christian Literature and Rhetoric* (Louisville: Westminster John Knox, 2003), 124.

7. Quintilian, *Institutio oratoria* 4.1.5: "The sole purpose of the *exordium* is to prepare our audience in such a way that they will be disposed to lend a ready ear to the rest of our speech." See Aune, *Westminster Dictionary*, 175.

8. The *narratio* was the second part of the ancient speech, which Cicero defines as "an exposition of events that have occurred or are supposed to have occurred" (*De inventione* 1.19.27). See Aune, *Westminster Dictionary*, 312.

9. For rhetorical analyses of Philippians, see Duane Watson, "A Rhetorical Analysis of Philippians and Its Implications for the Unity Question," *Novum Testamentum* 30

Establishing the Pastoral Vision (1:1–11): The exordium

As in all of the letters of Paul but unlike ancient hortatory letters in general, Paul writes to a community—to the "saints in Christ Jesus in Philippi with the bishops and deacons." Nothing else is said in the letter about the bishops and deacons, for Paul addresses the whole church. With the exception of one instance in which he addresses individuals in the church (4:2), he speaks to the whole community throughout the letter. Paul's pastoral theology was therefore primarily related to ecclesial concerns. His corporate concern is evident in his introductory thanksgiving, especially in his use of the plural "you" (1:5, 6, 9–11) and the repeated phrase "all of you" (1:4, 7 [twice]). As in the other letters, Paul's prayer offers an important indication of his central pastoral concerns as he reports on the content of his prayers. Paul moves from thanksgiving (1:3–6) to personal reflection (1:7–8) and petition (1:9–11), reporting on the content of his prayers, all of which refer to the entire community.

Paul's pastoral agenda is first evident when he explains the cause of his thanksgiving in 1:3–6. In recalling that he prays for the Philippians often (*pantote*) and that he does so with joy (1:4), he introduces a dominant theme in the letter.[10] Their "partnership [*koinōnia*] in the gospel from the first day until now" is the object of Paul's joy and the source of his thanksgiving.[11] As one whose task is "the defense and confirmation of the gospel" (1:7; cf. 1:16), Paul does not stand alone. This partnership includes not only the gifts that the Philippians have sent (4:15) but also their participation in his tribulations (*thlipsis*, 4:14),

---

(1988): 57–87. The *propositio* announces the case to be argued, whereas the *probatio* offers the proofs that support the main thesis. The purpose of the *peroratio* is to summarize the argument and influence the emotions. See Ben Witherington III, *Friendship and Finances in Philippi*, The New Testament in Context (Valley Forge, PA: Trinity Press International, 1994), 11–19. For Philippians as chiasmus, see A. Boyd Luter and Michelle V. Lee, "Philippians as Chiasmus: Key to the Structure, Unity, and Theme Questions," *New Testament Studies* 41 (1995): 89–101.

10. Cf. *chara* in Phil. 1:25; 2:2, 29; 4:1; *chairō* in 1:18; 2:17–18, 28; 3:1; 4:4, 10. Paul is the model for the outlook that he expects of the Philippians (3:1; 4:4–6).

11. Paul Holloway, *Consolation in Philippians: Philosophical Sources and Rhetorical Strategy* (Cambridge: Cambridge University Press, 2001), 89.

their prayers for him, and the partnership of love (2:1) that unites the community.[12] Indeed, the Philippians are "partners in my grace" (*synkoinōnoi mou tēs charitos*, 1:7; NRSV, "share in God's grace with me"). Whereas Paul expresses his gratitude for the love that binds him to the community in other letters (cf. 1 Thess. 1:3–5), here he indicates his thankfulness for a partnership that affects every aspect of Christian experience.

In describing his *koinōnia* with the Philippians, Paul signals the dominant concern of a letter that consistently evokes the language of friendship. According to Aristotle (*Ethica nichoma-chea* 8.12.1), *koinōnia* is the distinguishing feature of friendship. Friends share all things and are "one soul," looking to the interests of the other. In times of distress, a true friend demonstrates concern for the other.[13] In 1:7–8 and 4:10–20, Paul recalls the warm relationship that binds him to the Philippians. By recalling their past *koinōnia* with him (1:5), he lays the basis for the central appeal of the letter: for the Philippians to be of "one spirit, one soul," and to "have the same mind" (2:2; 4:2).

Here, as elsewhere in Paul's letters (cf. 1 Cor. 1:10–2:5; Gal. 1:6–9; 1 Thess. 1:5) and in friendship letters generally, Paul refers at the beginning of the discourse to the journey that he has already traveled with the community. This reference to the past journey will, no doubt, remind the Philippians of the common investment that he and the Philippians have made. In Phil. 1:6, Paul moves from the past journey to the prospects for the future—the issue that is in doubt. Paul's expression of confidence (*pepoithōs auto touto*) anticipates the frequent reference to his certainties in Philippians (cf. 1:25; 2:24)—certainties calculated to reassure the wavering community (cf. *oida* in 1:25). He also moves from the community's role (1:5) to God's activity (1:6), indicating that this certainty rests on his conviction about God: "He who began a good work will bring it to

12. G. W. Peterman, *Paul's Gift from Philippi: Conventions of Gift-Exchange and Christian Giving*, Society for New Testament Studies Monograph Series 92 (Cambridge: Cambridge University Press, 1997), 119–20.

13. Rainer Metzner, "In aller Freundschaft: Ein frühchristlicher Fall freundschaft-licher Gemeinschaft (Phil 2.25–30)," *New Testament Studies* 48 (2002): 112.

completion by the day of Jesus Christ." That is, Paul's work
among the Philippians has not come to an end, for God is the
primary actor in the drama. Paul uses the language "begin . . .
bring to completion" (*enarchomai . . . epiteleō*) elsewhere with
humans as the subject, demonstrating in those instances that
the completion of a task among humans is no certainty. Thus
he encourages the Corinthians to complete the collection that
they began a year ago (2 Cor. 8:10, 11), and he reprimands the
Galatians for beginning in the Spirit, only to end in the flesh
(Gal. 3:2). In Philippians, however, the subject is God. Paul
knows from the Hebrew Scriptures that God completes what
God begins. The same combination of the verbs *archomai . . .
epiteleō* appears in 1 Samuel 3:12, when God promises to bring
an end to the priestly line of Eli, saying (literally), "I begin [*archomai*] and I will bring to completion [*epitelesō*]." A similar
conviction is expressed in Numbers 23:19 (NRSV):

> God is not a human being, that he should lie,
> or a mortal, that he should change his mind.
> Has he promised, and will he not do it?
> Has he spoken, and will he not fulfill it?[14]

Paul's conviction rests on the frequent Old Testament affirmation of the faithfulness of God. In his pastoral role, he participates in God's work of bringing the community's narrative to
a conclusion.

This emphasis on God as the one who is present at the
beginning and draws to a conclusion echoes the emphasis
in Deutero-Isaiah, according to which God is the beginning
and the end (Isa. 41:4; 44:6; 48:12, 13) who will soon do a
"new thing" for Israel that is analogous to the primordial act
of creation (Isa. 42:5, 8–9). These words, spoken at a time
of corporate doubt about the future of the people of God,
now resonate in Paul's assurance to the Philippians. Creation
and redemption stand in relationship to each other, for the

14. See J. Gerald Janzen, "Creation and New Creation in Phil. 1:6," *Horizons in
Biblical Theology* 18 (1996): 36.

God who is active in the creation of the community will bring the church to completion.[15] The phrase "the one who began" (*ho enarxamenos*), which is parallel to "the first day" (Phil. 1:5–6), points to the church as God's "new creation" (2 Cor. 5:17). Here we note the parallel between Philippians 1:5 and 1:6:

> 1:5   first day until now.
>
> 1:6   first day until the day of Christ.

At the beginning of the letter, Paul establishes the narrative framework once-now-then.[16] The church participates in God's cosmic narrative, which has a beginning, a middle, and an end. At the beginning is the work of God: the one who "began a good work" at the foundation of the church (cf. "work" in 1:22; 2:30). The focus on God as the one who called the church into being is consistent with Paul's affirmations elsewhere that the church came into being by the power of God. The message came "not in word only but also in power and in the Holy Spirit" (1 Thess. 1:5). Paul first came to the Corinthians "with a demonstration of the Spirit and of power, so that your faith might rest not on human wisdom but on the power of God" (1 Cor. 2:4–5 NRSV).

Because it is a cosmic drama, Paul's imprisonment will not frustrate the eternal plan of God. Just as God is the beginning and end of everything, the church is now in the middle of a cosmic drama, standing between the beginning and the end. Paul's claim that God "has begun a good work" and will "bring it to completion" presupposes that God continues to be active in the formation of the community. God's creative activity did not reach its climax at the birth of the church; it "begins with the conversion of the sinner and lasts until the

15. Joachim Gnilka, *Der Philipperbrief*, Herders theologischer Kommentar zum Neuen Testament (Freiburg: Herder, 1980), 46.

16. See Troels Engberg-Pedersen, *Paul and the Stoics* (Louisville: Westminster John Knox, 2000), 86.

end."[17] His thanksgiving anticipates the words of Philippians 2:13: "It is God who is at work in you, enabling you both to will and to work for his good pleasure" (NRSV). At the end, God will transform the community "by the power that also enables him to make all things subject to himself" (3:21 NRSV). The church is making progress toward the eschaton, and God is active in this progress.

> The fundamental theological tactic of the letter's discourse interprets the Philippians' experience by means of a larger narrative about God, Christ, and Paul. The experience of community resulting from Paul's missionary work is part of a grand drama beginning with Christ's decision to live as a servant and reaching its goal with Christ's return. The letter treats the experience of the Philippians as a process and holds forth a clear goal that coincides with the resolution of the grand narrative. Paul describes the Philippian community as a good work that will be brought to completion on the day of Christ (1:6).[18]

A congregation is a work in progress. As in other passages, the focus is on God's work in calling the church into being.

Paul Schubert's observation that the thanksgivings have an "eschatological climax" is not merely a form critical insight.[19] It is a recognition that Paul's pastoral agenda is the eschatological completion of the work that God has initiated. Paul's pastoral theology begins with the acknowledgment that the church is God's creation, which God is bringing toward its goal. As Paul says in 1 Corinthians 1:8, "Who will confirm you to the end." As a work in progress, the community is empowered by God as it looks toward its goal. One may observe the frequency with which Paul emphasizes the eschatological dimension of God's

17. T. Laato, *Paulus und das Judentum: Anthropologische Erwägungen* (Åbo, Finland: Åbo Akademis Förlag, 1991), 202.

18. Stowers, "Friends and Enemies," 117.

19. Paul Schubert, *The Form and Function of the Pauline Thanksgivings*, Beihefte zur Zeitschrift für die neutestamentliche Wissenschaft 20 (Berlin: Töpelmann, 1939), 4.

work in Philippians. Paul indicates that his misfortunes will result in ultimate salvation as he awaits the hope. According to Philippians 3:20, the community awaits a Savior who will transform their body of lowliness and conform it to the Lord Jesus Christ with the energy of the one who subjects all things. In the meantime, the community waits in hope as God continues to work to fulfill his purpose.

In anticipation of the letter's deeply personal tone, Paul moves from God's role in the transformation of the Philippians to his own role as one who is deeply involved in God's work. This transition between the thanksgiving (1:3–6) and the petition for the Philippians' progress in 1:7–8 is not an interruption but a reflection of Paul's own involvement in the work of God for the transformation of the Philippians. "It is right for me to think this way [dikaion emoi touto phronein] about all of you" indicates the reciprocal nature of his relationship with them (hyper emou phronein, cf. 4:10). The language of intimacy anticipates 2:16–17 and recalls 2 Corinthians 7:3, "you are in our hearts, to die together and to live together." His statement that he "longs to see them" (Phil. 1:8) anticipates a later comment (4:1), "Therefore, my beloved brothers and sisters, whom I love and long for, my joy and my crown," indicating Paul's intimate familial relationship with the congregation. Paul speaks not as their ruler but as their "partner" (synkoinōnos, 1:7; cf. 4:10) in grace.[20] One may note the constant emphasis on "all of you" in 1:7–8 (cf. 1:3). His existence is intertwined with that of the congregation.

Just as Paul's expression of gratitude for the community in 1:3–6 indicates a pastoral vision, his petition in 1:9–11 indicates the goal of God's work. Paul's prayer gives specificity to the reference in 1:6 as he picks up the eschatological reference to the day of Christ. His prayer to God reaffirms his earlier comment that God is the one who brings the church to completion. One may note two purpose (hina) clauses that declare the two dimensions of Paul's prayer. In the first, he prays that "your

20. NRSV, "you share in God's grace."

love may overflow more and more with knowledge and full insight" (1:9 NRSV). In the second, he prays that they will be "pure and blameless" on the day of Christ (1:10). These petitions are related to each other insofar as the community can be blameless on the day of Christ only when it has advanced beyond the tensions of the moment (cf. 4:2–3) to the full abundance of love.

The first dimension of Paul's request focuses the attention on the continuing progress of the community. He assumes that a community not related by the ties of kinship will be bound by love. He acknowledges later that the "encouragement of love" (2:1) already exists within the community, but he adds the superlatives—not only to overflow (*perisseuein*) but to overflow more and more (cf. 1 Thess. 4:1, "abound more"). As in 1 Thessalonians 3:12, Paul's prayer is for the growth of love among the Philippians—something that progresses in time. Because the eschatological age is the age of abundance, as Paul accents with his consistent use of "overflow" (*perisseuein*),[21] love should overflow within the community.[22]

The frequency of his call for love in his instructions for his converts indicates that it is the single most important characteristic of these communities.[23] Whereas Paul most often encourages his communities to "love one another" (cf. Rom. 13:8; Gal. 5:13; 1 Thess. 3:12), here his concern is that the believers *love*; the focus is not "*whom* the Christian loves (and must love), but . . . the fact that he loves (and must love) with a heart that God's own love has transformed."[24] Wherever Paul elaborates on the meaning of love, he indicates that it consists

21. Cf. Rom. 5:15, "grace abounded"; Rom. 15:13, "so that you may abound in hope by the power of the Holy Spirit"; 1 Cor. 14:12, "so that you may excel"; 2 Cor. 1:5, "the sufferings of Christ and the consolation are abundant"; 3:9, "the ministry of justification abounds in glory."

22. A. Grabner-Haider, *Paraklese und Eschatologie bei Paulus* (Münster: Aschendorff, 1968), 139.

23. See R. Mohrlang, "Love," in *Dictionary of Paul and His Letters*, ed. G. F. Hawthorne and R. P. Martin (Downers Grove, IL: InterVarsity, 1993), 576.

24. T. J. Deidun, *New Covenant Morality in Paul*, Analecta biblica 89 (Rome: Biblical Institute Press, 1981), 144.

primarily of looking out for the interests of others within the community of faith.[25] In contrast to Paul's prayer for the increase in the community's love in 1 Thessalonians 3:12, in Philippians 1:9–10 Paul qualifies the nature of this love: "in knowledge and insight" (*en epignōsei kai pasē aisthēsei*).[26] He does not speak of love in a vague or emotional sense;[27] nor does he pray only for the increase of their love. Rather, he prays that their love will abound with particular qualities—"in knowledge and insight." That is, love acquires greater sensitivity as the believer matures. Paul's word for "insight" (*aisthēsis*) refers primarily to perception by the senses but takes on the metaphorical meaning of "sensitivity" or "insight."[28] Paul's appeal to cognition and sensitivity anticipates his subsequent call for a new mind-set (2:5), indicating that Christian progress entails an understanding of the nature of love.

The articular infinitive in 1:10 elaborates on the result of this progression. Believers may "determine the things that matter" (*dokimazein ta diapheronta*; NRSV, "determine what is best"). The description of the goal of Christian progress as the capacity to "determine the things that matter" is borrowed from Stoic ethics, according to which "the things that matter" (*ta diapheronta*) are distinguished from the things that do not (*ta adiaphora*).[29] His description of the goal of Christian progress

25. Note Paul's appeal to communal love in the context of discord. In Rom. 14:15 and 1 Cor. 8:1; 14:1, love is equated with seeking the interests of others. This theme is especially apparent in 1 Corinthians 13.

26. The prayer that their love abound in *epignōsis* is parallel to Paul's thanksgiving in Philem. 6, according to which Philemon has demonstrated a "knowledge of everything good" (*epignōsis pantos agathou*). One may compare the petition in Col. 1:9 ("we have not ceased praying that you may be filled with the full knowledge [*epignōsis*] of his will").

27. See Engberg-Pedersen, *Paul and the Stoics*, 109.

28. W. Bauer, F. W. Danker, W. F. Arndt, and F. W. Gingrich, *Greek-English Lexicon of the New Testament and Other Early Christian Literature*, 3d ed. (Chicago: University of Chicago Press, 1999), 29.

29. Ibid., 239. On the Stoic distinction, see James L. Jaquette, *Discerning What Counts: The Function of the adiaphora topos in Paul's Letters*, Society of Biblical Literature Dissertation Series 146 (Atlanta: Scholars Press, 1995). On Paul's view of what matters, see pp. 213–14.

appears to be an abbreviated description of the language that he develops later in Romans, where he describes both the humanity that is under the wrath of God and the humanity that results from the righteousness of God. Under the wrath of God, humans do not "see fit to acknowledge God" (*edokimasan ton theon echein en epignōsei*, Rom. 1:28). One who knows God's will and "determines what is best" (*dokimazeis ta diapheronta*) does not, in fact, keep God's commandments (Rom. 2:18).

In contrast to those who claim to "determine what is best" without living up to this standard, Paul encourages the community of faith to "discern the will of God—what is good and acceptable and perfect" (Rom. 12:2). In Romans Paul presents a similar ethical vision, contrasting those who do not have God in full knowledge with the ethical ideal of those who "test the better things" (2:18). The Christian community is called upon to live up to this ideal in Romans 12:1–2. Paul then describes this existence in Romans 12–15. Thus the prayer in Philippians 1:9–11 is an abbreviated form of Paul's ethical ideal. Although he uses Stoic categories, he defines the categories in his own terms. Indeed, in the central section of the epistle, Paul develops the theme of the things that matter.

In the parallel purpose clause in 1:10b–11, Paul focuses on the end result, elaborating on the reference to the day of Christ in 1:6. God will have completed his work when the community is "pure and blameless on the day of Christ, filled with the harvest of righteousness through Jesus Christ to the glory and praise of God." That is, the ethical progression by which the community abounds in love will be evident in its capacity to determine the things that matter and will result in the community's blamelessness on the day of Christ. The petition indicates the central place of Paul's pastoral theology of transformation. His church stands between its progress from the first day and the ultimate day of Christ. This pastoral vision determines Paul's ministry, for in the remainder of the letter Paul presents himself as a model and offers ethical instructions that will lead to the church's ultimate transformation.

Paul as a Model of Christian Conduct (1:12–26): The narratio

Having prayed for the transformation of the community, in 1:12–26 Paul writes to persuade the listeners that recent events (*ta kat' eme*) will not frustrate his pastoral vision, and he offers himself as a model for the outlook that he wants them to adopt. Paul is confident that recent events will, in fact, result in progress (*prokopē*) for the gospel (1:12; NRSV, "spread the gospel") and progress (*prokopē*) for the Philippians (1:25). In the repetition "In this I rejoice . . . I will continue to rejoice" (*en toutō chairō, alla kai charēsomai*, 1:18), Paul exhibits the rejoicing in the midst of distress that he asks of his readers (3:1; 4:4). The two expressions of joy point backward (1:12–18a) and forward (1:18b–26) respectively, indicating the two reasons that Paul is not deterred by present circumstances. The present tense "In this I rejoice" (*en toutō chairō*) points to the ongoing events in Paul's ministry—the fact that the gospel is advancing and Christ is being preached (1:12–18a). The future "I will rejoice" (*charēsomai*) points to the future hope expressed in 1:18b–26. The events will "turn out to salvation" (cf. Job 13:16) according to Paul's expectation and hope, for he will not be ashamed and Christ will be manifest. In keeping with the prayer for God's purposes to be fulfilled at the day of Christ (Phil. 1:6, 10), Paul points to his own eschatological vision.

Interpreters have mistakenly placed the emphasis either on the opposition to Paul or on his understanding of eschatology. The focus is, rather, on Paul's certainty, as indicated by the repetition of "I know" (*oida*, 1:19, 25). Over against the uncertainty raised by his imprisonment, Paul knows one thing: he will participate in their progress (1:25). Thus the prayer expressed in 1:9–11 has not been frustrated. Paul's ministry will participate in their advancement and joy. The result will be that "your boast [will] abound in me" (1:26). That is, their progress is bound up with Paul's presence, and their boasting in Christ will abound through Paul's presence (1:26; cf. 1 Cor.

1:31; 2 Cor. 10:17). The nature of this progress becomes evident in the argument that follows.

Living Worthily of the Gospel: The propositio (1:27–30)

Although Paul in 1:26 assures the Philippians of his future presence, the series of imperatives in 1:27–2:18 calls for a conduct "worthy of the gospel" (1:27) whether he is absent or present (1:27; 2:12). The *inclusio* of 1:27–30 and 4:1–3 focuses the attention on the community's role in transformation. At the beginning of the unit, Paul indicates that for them to conduct themselves in a manner "worthy of the gospel of Christ" is to "stand in one spirit" (1:27); at the conclusion to this unit, he says, "Therefore stand in the Lord" (4:1). Near the beginning of this unit, Paul encourages the readers to have "one spirit" and "one soul" (1:27) and to "mind the same thing" (*hina to auto phronēte*, 2:2); at the end he encourages Euodia and Syntyche to "be of the same mind" (*to auto phronein*, 4:2). Between these two calls for unity, Paul lays the foundation for his call to "stand in the Lord" and "have the same mind," describing this existence in the language of transformation.

The opening imperative in 1:27 introduces the *propositio* for the entire letter. The progress of the church (1:25) will be evident insofar as the members conduct themselves as citizens of the heavenly commonwealth. The verb *politeuesthe* (literally "discharge your obligations as citizens") anticipates the noun *politeuma* ("citizenship") in 3:20; thus a political metaphor frames the entire discussion. The community's *politeuma* in heaven shapes the nature of its conduct as it awaits the ultimate transformation (3:21). In the meantime, as the waiting community lives out its citizenship in an alternative commonwealth, it evokes the hostility of its own society (1:28–29). In the context of the forces that threaten the community (1:28–29), Paul encourages the Philippians to stand together as in a military formation and to share his struggle (1:30). In describing the conduct of the citizens of the heavenly *politeuma* (2:1–3:21), Paul develops the theme of unity in 1:27–30 in the remainder of the letter, alternating between imperatives for communal living and models of this transformation to describe the existence that he introduces in the opening thanksgiving (1:10–11). The emphasis on standing and struggling together against opposition elaborates on the prayer for discerning love in 1:10–11.

Making the Case for Unity: The probatio (2:1–4:3)

The second imperative, *plērōsate mou tēn charan* ("Make full my joy," 2:2), once more reflects Paul's pastoral ambition of playing a role in the formation of the community and his conviction that his churches are his "boast" and "joy" at the end (cf. 2:16; 1 Thess. 2:19). By looking not to their own interests but to the interests of others, they will complete his joy and demonstrate the progress indicated in the opening petition. The third imperative, *touto phroneite en hymin* ("Have this mind in you," 2:5), further clarifies the nature of Christian formation and introduces the narrative of Christ, who exemplifies the conduct of living out the heavenly citizenship. In giving up the form of God for the form of a slave, he is the model for looking to the interests of others (2:3).

The narrative of 2:6–11 introduces the qualities of transformation that Paul inculcates in his listeners. We see here the nature of the Christian formation in the central section of the letter as Paul moves from the story of Christ (2:6–11) to the instructions for the community (2:12–18) and follows with examples of the alternative existence from Timothy and Epaphroditus (2:19–30) and from Paul's own life (3:2–21). Paul's use of forms of *morph-* indicates the significance of transformation in this letter. In 2:6–11, Paul depicts the "mind of Christ" as the narrative of the one who gave up the "form [*morphē*] of God" for the "form [*morphēn*] of a slave" in a supreme act of self-sacrifice before God exalted him (2:9–11). Paul's desire to "be like him [*symmorphizomenos*] in his death" (3:10) indicates his role in the transformation. As the repetition of forms of *morph-* indicates, the language of transformation provides the structure of the passage. The transformation of

Christ becomes the model for Paul (3:2–16) and for Christians, who will also be transformed (cf. *symmorphon*, 3:21).

One dimension of transformation is evident in the fourth and fifth imperatives of 2:12–18, in Paul's description of the impact of the Christian narrative. "Therefore" (*hōste*, 2:12) indicates that the Christian story is the basis for the demands that follow. Just as Christ "became obedient to death" (2:8), the community has always obeyed (2:12). Paul's instruction *tēn heautōn sōtērian katergazesthe* ("Work out your own salvation," 2:12) challenges the community to continue its obedience and participate in the work that God is doing (cf. 1:6). This imperative must be understood in the context of the previous demand to adopt the "mind of Christ" (2:5), which is depicted in the story of Christ in 2:6–11. Paul speaks to the entire community, calling for a corporate self-sacrifice modeled on the selflessness of Christ. The plural reference to "your own salvation" maintains the emphasis on corporate eschatological salvation, as in 1:6, 10–11.[30] Just as the exaltation of Christ followed his self-emptying, the church's corporate self-sacrifice results in its salvation.[31] Here Paul insists that the community has a role in the salvation that God will ultimately bring to completion. The community's opponents are destined for destruction, but the church is destined for salvation (1:28). The salvation to which the community aspires is the completion of God's work "on the day of Christ" (cf. 1:6, 11).

In 2:13 Paul places the imperatives in context, indicating that God is the one who is at work. Here he completes the thought of 1:6. The God who began a good work and will bring it to completion is now at work in the community. This affirmation is consistent with Paul's understanding elsewhere (cf. 1 Thess. 2:12–13), and it reflects Paul's own experience of being able to "do all things through Christ who strengthens me" (Phil.

30. See W. Schenk, *Der Philipperbrief des Paulus* (Stuttgart: Kohlhammer, 1984), 217. The reflexive pronoun *heautōn* emphasizes the reciprocal nature of the communal response.

31. Beat Weber, "Philipper 2,12–13: Text–Context–Intertext," *Biblische Notizen* 85 (1996): 33.

4:13). If God were not active in the midst of the community's struggle against opposition (1:28), the community would not survive.[32] Just as God exalted the one who sacrificed himself (2:9–11), God now empowers the community. The community is active in working out its corporate salvation because God empowers it to live the transformed existence. God is active "to will and to work [*to thelein kai to poiein*] for his good pleasure" (2:13).

The final imperative in this unit, *panta poieite chōris gongysmōn kai dialogismōn* ("Do all things without murmuring or arguing," 2:14), reinforces the consistent focus on unity within the community and contrasts the church with Israel's conduct in the wilderness when it was a "crooked and perverse generation" (Deut. 32:5), "murmuring" against Moses.[33] Instead, Paul challenges the community to distinguish itself by the opposite conduct to be "blameless and innocent [*amemptoi kai akeraioi*], children of God without blemish [*amōma*] in the midst of a crooked and perverse generation" (Phil. 2:15 NRSV).[34] The distinguishing features of the community now are parallel to the description of the eschatological people of God as "pure and blameless" (in 1:10) on the day of Christ. Here Paul's understanding of transformation is evident as he challenges the church members to be in the present what he hopes they will be on the day of Christ. Already they are a counterculture that "shines in the world." That is, those who live out their heavenly citizenship already show the signs of transformation. Not only does he pray for the community's blamelessness on the day of Christ (1:10); here he describes a community that already demonstrates the qualities that he elsewhere hopes to see in

32. See Stephen Fowl, *The Story of Christ in the Ethics of Paul*, Journal for the Study of the New Testament: Supplement Series 36 (Sheffield, Eng.: JSOT Press, 1990), 97.

33. See Exod. 15–17 and Num. 14–17 for the complaints of the people of Israel in the desert wandering. Paul refers to Israel's grumbling also in 1 Cor. 10:11. In Hellenistic Judaism it became a characteristic of life in opposition to God (cf. Sir. 10:25; 46:7; *Psalms of Solomon* 5:15; 16:11). Schenk, *Philipperbrief*, 220.

34. The purpose clause introduced by *hina* has imperative force. Schenk, *Philipperbrief*, 220.

the church at the parousia (cf. 1 Thess. 3:13). In Phil. 1:10, he says, "that you may be [ēte]" blameless on the day of Christ; here he says, "that you may become [genēsthe]" blameless. According to 2:16, however, the church is unfinished business. The phrase "that I can boast on the day of Christ" (eis kauchēma emoi eis hēmeran Christou) recalls Paul's earlier reference in the prayer at 1:10. They will be his "boast" (kauchēma, cf. 2 Cor. 1:14). One may note that Paul is their "boast" (kauchēma) in 1:26. This theme is also present in 1 Thessalonians 2:19–20. The clarifying words "that I did not run in vain" (Phil. 2:16) is a familiar Pauline phrase (cf. Gal. 2:2; 1 Thess. 3:5). Paul assumes the role of the servant of Isaiah 49:4. His ministerial vocation is fulfilled only in the transformation of believers as he pours himself out as a libation (2:17). Believers are shaped by the story of Christ.

Here one sees Paul's vision for ministry. In keeping with the prayer that "their love may increase," Paul describes a love that is shaped by the community's foundational narrative of the self-emptying of Christ. To live out the heavenly citizenship is to be a community in which members do not look to their own interests but to the interests of others. Just as Christ gave up the form of God for the form of a slave before his exaltation, the church is composed of individuals whose lives become conformed to the foundational story. This transformation will result in the blamelessness of the community on the day of Christ. That is, he became what we are that we might become what he is.[35] The success of his ministry rests on the transformation of the people, which occurs when the community identifies with the one who did not look to his own interests but to the interests of others.

In the examples that follow, Paul offers models of the transformed existence for which he has prayed, contrasting the models with others who do not exhibit the transformed existence.

35. See Morna D. Hooker, "A Partner in the Gospel: Paul's Understanding of His Ministry," in *Theology and Ethics in Paul and His Interpreters*, ed. Eugene H. Lovering Jr. and Jerry Sumney (Nashville: Abingdon, 1996), 90, for the importance of "interchange" in Paul's theology. See pp. 25–26.

Whereas "all of them are seeking their own interests" (2:21), Timothy cares for the Philippians (2:20), and Epaphroditus "risked his life" (2:30) in his work with the Philippians. In contrast to those who boast in the flesh, Paul is also a model of transformation. In 3:2–16 he provides the basis for the encouragement in 4:1, "Stand firm in the Lord." Paul is the model (3:17) of the narrative existence that the Philippians experience, for he stands between the radical change in his life that has already occurred (3:2–11) and his ultimate goal. Like the Philippians, he stands in the "now" between past and future, having given up all things for the sake of Christ (3:2–11) but not yet made perfect (3:12–14); between being "conformed to his death" and the resurrection of the dead (3:10–11). In the present moment, as he knows the "partnership of his sufferings," he also knows "the power of his resurrection." Thus now, as one living between the times, he presses on, empowered by God. Having lost everything in order to attain the ultimate goal, he incorporates the Christ hymn into his existence.[36] He is the model for the Philippians (3:17), who are also faced with destructive alternative models (3:18–19). In contrast to those whose god is the belly and whose end is destruction, the Philippians await the ultimate transformation. Having been conformed to the narrative of the Christ who emptied himself, the Philippians await the time when Christ will "transform the body of our humiliation that it may be conformed to the body of his glory, by the power that also enables him to make all things subject to himself" (3:20–21 NRSV). The power of God mentioned in 1:6 will complete the task of transforming the community. Those who are conformed to the dying of Christ will ultimately be transformed.

The church is oriented to its heavenly citizenship, awaiting the day of Christ, when he will change our body of lowliness to be conformed to the body of his glory. As Christians are transformed by the cross, they await the ultimate transformation.

---

36. Gerald Hawthorne, "The Imitation of Christ: Philippians," in *Patterns of Discipleship in the New Testament*, ed. Richard N. Longenecker (Grand Rapids: Eerdmans, 1996), 174.

The story of Jesus' change of "form" (*morphē*) and Paul's model of being "conformed to the cross" is the pattern of self-denial. For those who make progress in discerning love, Christ "will transform [*metaschēmatisei*] the body of our humiliation that it may be conformed [*symmorphon*] to the body of his glory." Those who are presently shaped by the narrative of Christ will receive the ultimate transformation.

Summing Up the Case for Transformation: The peroratio (4:4–20)

In the concluding section of the letter, Paul encourages the Philippians to practice the transformed existence (4:4–8) and offers himself as a model of transformation (4:9–20), thus summarizing the earlier parts of the letter. In 4:4, Paul reiterates the theme of joy (cf. 3:1), and in 4:5–7 he pleads for the conduct that is consistent with the qualities that he called for in the letter's *propositio* (1:27–30).[37] The "thank-you note" in 4:10–20 summarizes themes of the letter, as Paul again refers to the Philippians' partnership (*koinōnia*, cf. 1:5) with him and offers himself as a model of one who remains undaunted in the context of difficult circumstances (4:10–13; cf. 1:12–18). Indeed, the Philippians have already demonstrated the transforming effects of the gospel by their sacrificial giving, which is a pleasing sacrifice to God (4:18). Nevertheless, Paul concludes the letter in the same way that he began: with a prayer that God will continue to work in the Philippians (4:19–20; cf. 1:9–11), filling them with all that they need.

Philippians as Pastoral Theology

Philippians offers a comprehensive look at Paul's understanding of transformation as the basis for his pastoral work. The moral life consists of the church's progression in love, which is evident as members look to the interests of others. Christians

37. See Witherington, *Friendship and Finances*, 111.

adopt the mind of Christ as they identify with the crucified one, who did not look out for himself. The increase in love, about which Paul prays, occurs when Christians are formed by the crucified Christ in anticipation of being transformed by the glorified Christ. Paul's ministry will reach its goal only when Christians, who are now being formed by the story of the crucified one, are ultimately transformed at the coming of Christ (3:21).

Paul's Pastoral Vision in 1 Thessalonians

In 1 Thessalonians, as in Philippians, Paul presents the congregation as part of a narrative that has a beginning, a middle, and an end. At the beginning, Paul's message came to the Thessalonians "in power and in the Holy Spirit" (1 Thess. 1:5), and the Thessalonians "received the word with joy inspired by the Holy Spirit" (1:6 NRSV). After the Thessalonians "turned to God from idols" (1:9), they became models of faithfulness throughout Macedonia and Achaia. In those early days, Paul had been like a father, "urging and encouraging . . . and pleading" (*parakalountes . . . paramythoumenoi kai martyromenoi*) with the Thessalonians to "lead a life worthy of God" (1 Thess. 2:12 NRSV). After receiving Timothy's positive report, Paul continues the conversation with this church, writing this pastoral letter. The outcome of the story is the destiny of Christians on the day of Christ (2:19; 3:11–13; 5:1–11).[38] In the more immediate future, he hopes to see the community (2:17). The letter is the middle point of the narrative.

The narrative quality of the Christians' existence is evident in 1 Thessalonians 1–3, which consists of Paul's prayers of thanksgiving interspersed with his narrative of the events leading up to the letter. Paul's thanksgiving in 1:2–10, 2:13–16, and 3:9–10 is followed by his petition in 3:11–13. His pastoral vision is most evident in his prayers, which depict the continuity

38. John W. Simpson, "Shaped by the Stories: Narrative in 1 Thessalonians," *Asbury Theological Journal* 53 (1998): 5.

between past, present, and future. He easily moves between thanksgiving and narrative because his thanksgivings reflect on his past relationship with the readers. His movement from thanksgiving (1:2–5) to the memory of the Thessalonians' reception of the Christian message (1:6–10) forms the opening thanksgiving, which introduces the basic themes of the letter and functions as the *exordium* of Paul's message. In chapters 2 and 3 Paul's description of past events in the Thessalonian church forms the *narratio* of the letter, setting the stage for Paul's argument for future conduct in chapters 4 and 5. The alternation of narrative and thanksgiving indicates that recent events are the background to his expression of thanksgiving in 2:13 and 3:9. Paul's defense of his conduct in 2:1–12 is the basis for the thanksgiving in 2:13,[39] and his thanksgiving in 3:9–10 is the result of the favorable report that Timothy has delivered.

The community lives in the "now" between the early days and the ultimate future. The first three chapters express gratitude for the Thessalonians' progress from the time that they "received the word" (2:13; cf. 1:5–10) until the moment when Paul writes 1 Thessalonians. As in Philippians, Paul indicates his pastoral vision first in his expressions of gratitude. In keeping with Paul's normal adaptation of the thanksgiving to the topic of the letter, he expresses gratitude for their progress—"work of faith and labor of love and steadfastness of hope" (1:3)—in response to Timothy's favorable report of their "faith and love" (3:6). In referring to their "labor of love," Paul maintains his consistent emphasis on love as the bond of communal existence.[40]

Despite the Thessalonians' progress, the church is unfinished business. As in Philippians, the community is his "joy and crown of boasting before the Lord at his parousia" (2:19). Paul makes the transition to the future in 3:9–10 with his request

39. See Jan Lambrecht, "Thanksgivings in 1 Thessalonians 1–3," in *The Thessalonians Debate*, ed. Karl P. Donfried and Johannes Beutler (Grand Rapids: Eerdmans, 2000), 146.
40. Cf. Gal. 5:6, "Neither circumcision nor uncircumcision matters, but faith working through love."

that he see the Thessalonians once more so that he can "restore what is lacking" in their faith (3:10), and in his exhortation he challenges them to "put on the breastplate of faith and love, and for a helmet the hope of salvation . . . through our Lord Jesus Christ" (5:8–9 NRSV). Thus the community's narrative concerns progress that is defined by faith, hope, and love.

The petition in 3:10 marks the turning point in the letter. Whereas Paul reports on his prayers in 3:9–10, he actually prays in 3:11–13. Paul's petition in 3:11–13 offers an insight into his understanding of Christian transformation. In parallel clauses he prays that "our God and Father himself and our Lord Jesus direct our way to you" and that "the Lord make you increase and abound in love for one another and for all, just as we abound in love for you" (NRSV). The petition indicates the close relationship between the activity of God, who is the active agent in the church's transformation, and Paul's own work (cf. Phil. 1:7–8). The first petition continues the thought of 1 Thessalonians 3:10; Paul's coming will be beneficial for the Thessalonians' Christian progress. The second petition, with its emphasis on love, is closely parallel to the petition in Philippians 1:10–11. After acknowledging the community's progress in loving one another (1 Thess. 1:3–5), he prays for the continuing abundance of their love. As in Philippians 1:10–11, Christian transformation occurs when love for one another "abounds" (*perisseusai*, 1 Thess. 3:12). Paul employs the synonymous words "increase and abound" for emphasis.[41] Again, God is the one who is active.

In contrast to the petition in Philippians 1:9–11, where the focus is on the nature of love, the petition here indicates the specific object of love: "to one another and to all" (1 Thess. 3:12). The petition that the believers love one another is consistent with Paul's frequent instructions to love those within the community of faith. The "neighbor" of Leviticus 19:18 is the person within the community (cf. Rom. 13:8–10; Gal.

41. See Malherbe, *Letters to the Thessalonians*, 212. For this redundancy, cf. also Rom. 5:20; 2 Cor. 4:15.

5:13–14). Consequently, the constant theme for Paul's exhortations is to "love one another" (cf. Rom. 12:10; 1 Thess. 4:9). We may also note Paul's regular use of "one another" to signify the community's communal concern (Rom. 14:13, 19; 15:5, 7, 14; 16:16; 2 Cor. 7:5; Gal. 5:13, 15; Phil. 2:3). Paul's prayer anticipates his instructions to "love one another" (1 Thess. 4:9) and to "build one another up" (4:18; 5:11).

The prayer that their love extend "to one another and to all" anticipates the instruction in 5:15 to "do good to one another and to all." The extension of Christian care to the wider community is unusual in Paul. In 1 Thessalonians he is aware of the sharp distinction between insiders and outsiders (cf. 4:12), and he knows the tenuous situation of the church within its society. The result, according to the clause in 3:11, is that God will establish their "hearts blameless in holiness before God and our Lord at the parousia of the Lord Jesus with all his saints." Having kept before the church the eschatological vision of God's ultimate future (1:9–10; 2:19), he prays that the ultimate result of the community's growth in love might be the blamelessness of the community at the coming of Christ. He has already sent Timothy to "establish" (*stērixai*, 3:2) the church; now he continues the prayer with the petition that God "establish their hearts" (3:13). This eschatological vision defines Paul's ministry, as he indicates in 2:19. His prayer that they may be blameless at the parousia is parallel to the petition in Philippians 1:10 that they be "pure and blameless at the day of Christ." Here Paul adds the words "in holiness" (*en hagiōsynē*), introducing a major theme of the letter (cf. 1 Thess. 4:3, 7). The advancement of the qualities of love in 3:12 defines the nature of holiness.

The content of the prayer is the transition to the paraenesis in chapters 4 and 5. The introduction to the paraenesis in 4:1–2 is the *propositio*, which states the case to be argued: that the Thessalonians are to "abound" in what they have been doing already. Whereas the prayer indicates the divine role in the community's formation, the paraenesis indicates the community's role in living "worthily" of God (cf. 2:12). The holiness for which Paul prays becomes evident in the specific aspects of the community's response in 4:3–5:11, which functions as the *probatio* of the argument, laying out the nature of the sanctification for which Paul had prayed (3:11–13). Paul instructs the community to avoid the sexual sins of the Gentiles (4:3, 8) and encourages the community's love for each other (4:9–12), developing the theme of communal love from 1:2–3 and 3:11. His eschatological reflections in 4:13–5:11 point the community toward the goal of their existence at the eschaton and serve as an exhortation for mutual edification (4:18; 5:11).

The final words to the Thessalonians, which reiterate Paul's call for the corporate ethical response that gives concreteness to the community's sanctification, function as the letter's *peroratio*. The support of leaders (5:12) and the help for all within the community (5:14–22) are expressions of the love that defines its existence. The fact that the instructions in 4:1–5:22 are framed by Paul's prayer for sanctification in 3:11–13 and the benediction in 5:23, "May the God of peace himself sanctify you entirely" (*autos de ho theos tēs eirēnēs hagiasai hymas holoteleis*), suggests that sanctification entails the community's ethical transformation as members abstain from sexual immorality (4:1–8) and demonstrate their faithfulness and love (4:9–5:22).[42] Although Paul calls for the community's response, the prayers indicate that God is at work (cf. 2:13) to effect the community's sanctification. In two clauses of the benediction, Paul reiterates his pastoral vision, placing special emphasis on the totality of the community's change. Although God has already called them to sanctification (4:3, 8; cf. 1 Cor. 1:2; 6:11), he prays that God will sanctify them "entirely" (*holoteleis*)[43] and that their spirit, soul, and body[44] will

42. Holtz, *Der erste Brief an die Thessalonicher*, 264.

43. The term was sometimes associated with a fully formed embryo. Aetius, in Pseudo-Plutarch, *De placita philosophorum* 5.21 (Herman Diels, *Doxographi graeci* [Berlin: W. de Gruyter, 1929], 433, a21), cited in Malherbe, *Letters to the Thessalonians*, 338.

44. In no other text does Paul use this tripartite division to describe the human. Because Paul uses a variety of formulae (e.g., "flesh and spirit," "mind and body"), we cannot conclude that this division reflects Paul's anthropology.

be "sound" (holoklēron)[45] and "blameless" (amemptōs, cf. 1 Thess. 3:13; Phil. 2:16) at the parousia.

Paul's adaptation of the expected form of the peace benediction results in a closing epistolary formula that summarizes the call to holy living that has characterized the entire letter.[46] The community's narrative therefore extends from the time that they "turned to God from idols" (1 Thess. 1:9) to the end, when they will be fully transformed. Paul's affirmation in 5:24, "The one who calls you is faithful, and he will do this," is parallel to the assurance in Philippians 1:6 that God will complete the work that God has begun. Thus Paul prays for God's transforming work and expresses confidence in the faithfulness of God in bringing the community to completion. Paul's pastoral theology in Philippians and 1 Thessalonians is both corporate and eschatological, as we have seen. As the founder of churches, he prays that God will work within communities so that they may be ready for the day of Christ. In the meantime, he continues to minister to his converts because his churches are an unfinished work. He envisions a transformation of his converts from their individual concerns to familial love. Paul is confident that God will complete the work that God began when the communities first accepted the gospel. As a nurse (1 Thess. 2:7) and father (2:12) to his churches, his role is to be the instrument of their transformation. The community that lives faithfully will be Paul's "crown" (2:19) at the parousia.

The surprising feature of Paul's prayer is his use of the language of holiness, which he takes from Israel's own experience of being separate from the nations (cf. Lev. 19:2). Paul applies this important category to a Gentile community in order to suggest the countercultural nature of its existence. He envi-

---

45. The word is used for limbs that have been mended; Bauer, Danker, Arndt, and Gingrich, Greek-English Lexicon, 703. It can also be used in cultic contexts for the flawlessness of the sacrifice and of the one offering the sacrifice; Holtz, Der erste Brief an die Thessalonicher, 265.

46. Jeffrey A. D. Weima, "'How You Must Walk to Please God': Holiness and Discipleship in 1 Thessalonians," in Patterns of Discipleship in the New Testament, ed. Richard N. Longenecker (Grand Rapids: Eerdmans, 1996), 101.

sions this Gentile church as the renewed Israel with the same cohesive moral identity that God required of Israel in the Old Testament.

Conclusion: Transformation and Pastoral Theology

Paul's portrayal of a community that lives in the "now" between God's creative act of establishing the community and the "day of Christ" is a constant feature in his letters and the central feature of his pastoral theology. We have seen in Philippians and 1 Thessalonians that Paul's pastoral ambition for the church defines his ministry. In his prayers he articulates a vision of the ultimate outcome of God's work and the community's progress toward that goal. In his statements about his own ministry, he indicates that his pastoral ambition is to work with God toward the completion of God's work. Paul's exhortations provide the specific examples of the transformed existence that will lead toward the goal. His pastoral work is determined by the fact that the church is unfinished business.

Paul's goal is the transformation of the community that will turn from self-centeredness to a corporate existence shaped primarily by the love exhibited by the self-denial of Jesus. In both Philippians and 1 Thessalonians, Paul assumes that the church actually does the will of God insofar as it is empowered "to will and to do" (Phil. 2:13). His reassurance that God is at work in the ethical transformation (Phil. 1:6) and his petition for God to act within the community (1 Thess. 3:11–13) indicate that Paul acknowledges no internal struggle as the community is transformed by God. Paul is the model of transformation. As he shares the sufferings of Christ, he denies himself for the sake of his communities and is empowered by the resurrection (Phil. 3:10), offering an example of the transformed behavior that he expects of his congregations. The success or failure of the communities to be transformed determines whether he has run in vain.

Paul's pastoral theology, which is largely ignored in contemporary conversations about the nature of the ministry, offers valuable insights for our own understanding. He challenges the individualism of our culture by insisting on a corporate understanding of the Christian faith. He envisions a community composed of people from a variety of backgrounds who are brought together by a shared story of the one who gave himself for others and who are sustained by the constant reminder of this narrative. As he articulates the goals of his ministry through his prayers, he offers insights for the outcome of our own work. If we adopt the Pauline understanding, we will work with God for church growth that consists of an increase in ethical sensitivity and care for others within the community. We will challenge the self-centeredness of our own society, measuring our effectiveness by the community's capacity to live in harmony with each other.

3

Living between the Times

Pauline Anthropology and the Problem of Transformation in Galatians

In Philippians Paul presents a confident expectation that God will complete what he began with the church, arguing that God now empowers the community "to will and to do" (2:13). He offers the ringing assurance that "the one who began a good work . . . will bring it to completion by the day of Jesus Christ" (1:6 NRSV). In both 1 Thessalonians and Philippians, Paul prays for the community's transformation (Phil. 1:9–11; 1 Thess. 3:13; 5:23) and assures the community of the divine power at work in its midst to bring it to completion (Phil. 2:13; 1 Thess. 2:13). In this way, they will be his "boast" at the return of Christ (Phil. 2:16; 1 Thess. 2:19). That is, the completion of this task is the test of his ministry—whether he has run "in vain" (Phil. 2:16; 1 Thess. 3:5). These two letters are distinguished by a confident expectation of the transformation of the community by the power of God. Paul's labor in the work that God is doing defines Paul's ministry.

In other letters Paul confronts the obstacles to the completion of God's work among the churches, and he speaks with less confidence about the ultimate success of his work. In those letters one finds no ringing assurance that God will complete the work that God has begun, as in Philippians 1:6. We shall consider here the obstacles to human transformation, especially in Galatians. As in Philippians and 1 Thessalonians, Paul observes in Galatians the narrative nature of Christian existence, reflecting on its past, present, and future. Although the church began well, the future is in doubt. In place of his expression of hope that at the end he will not have run in vain (Phil. 2:16), in Galatians he says, "I fear that I have run in vain" (4:11). In place of the affirmation that "it is God who is at work in you, enabling you both to will and to work for his good pleasure" (Phil. 2:13 NRSV), Paul speaks of a battle of flesh against spirit "to prevent you from doing what you want" (Gal. 5:17). In the context of battle, Paul presents a more complex picture of the challenges of human transformation and the capacity to do what one wills. Because of this complicating factor, we now see a new dimension to Paul's pastoral theology as he suffers the pains of childbirth among the Galatians in his desire to effect Christian formation (4:19). Paul's pastoral theology becomes evident in his attempt to complete the community's narrative. We will explore here the challenges to Christian formation and the significance of these challenges for Paul's pastoral theology.

The Pastoral Situation in Galatians

Paul's description of the Galatian situation reveals the challenges facing the transformation of the community, for Galatians is a response to the community's relapse. Instead of the confident expectation that God will complete what God began (Phil. 1:6), in Galatians 3:3–4 Paul asks, "Having started with the Spirit, are you now ending with the flesh? Did you experience so much for nothing?" (NRSV). Paul speaks consistently of the church's good beginning and its abandonment of the good news brought by Paul. As distant readers of this conversation, we are limited in our knowledge of the pastoral situation, for we know it only from Paul's comments and from our reconstruction of the probable course of events. We also do not know how much Paul knew about the opposition. We need not engage in extended mirror reading that assumes that every argument of Paul is a counterargument to the position of the opponents. We can distinguish (a) what is certain about Paul's understanding; (b) what is highly probable; and (c) what is likely about the situation.[1] What is certain is that opponents have come to the Galatians offering what Paul calls "another gospel" (1:6). Paul does not name the opponents but describes them as "those who are confusing you" (1:7) and "those who unsettle you" (5:12). They believe that Jesus was Israel's Messiah but demand that the Galatians follow at least some of the law, especially the ritual requirement of circumcision (6:12). Paul not only accuses them of perverting the gospel of Christ (1:7); he questions their motives also (6:12).[2]

Since Jews had traditionally welcomed Gentiles into Israel by insisting that they keep the Torah, it is probable that the opponents of Paul were Jewish Christians who insisted that the converts adhere to the traditional entrance requirements for Gentiles. The fact that Jewish literature appealed to Abraham as the example of the first proselyte suggests that Paul's argument about Abraham in Galatians 3 is his response to the opponents' interpretation of the same story.[3] The "everlasting covenant" of circumcision (Gen. 17:1–14), which God established with Abraham and his descendants, was the basis for the opponents' insistence that those who are included as Abraham's children must be circumcised.

1. John M. G. Barclay, "Mirror-Reading a Polemical Letter: Galatians as a Test Case," *Journal for the Study of the New Testament* 31 (1987): 88–89.

2. Ben Witherington III, *Grace in Galatia: A Commentary on Paul's Letter to the Galatians* (Grand Rapids: Eerdmans, 1998), 25.

3. Cf. Philo, *On the Virtues* 175–186; H. Moxnes, *Theology in Conflict: Studies in Paul's Understanding of God in Romans* (Edinburgh: T. & T. Clark, 1980), 130.

The Galatians apparently accepted the arguments of the outsiders that, in order to be Abraham's children, they must be circumcised (5:2; 6:12–13) and be faithful to the Torah (cf. 4:10). Paul's assurance that the law can be fulfilled through the power of the Spirit (5:13–6:10) suggests the likelihood that the Galatians were attracted to the Jewish law as a means of gaining self-control. Paul accuses them of "deserting" the one who called them by the gospel (1:6),[4] of turning again to the idolatry that had characterized their previous existence (4:8–9), and of "falling away from grace" (5:4). Although he fears that he has run "in vain" (4:11), he writes the letter to persuade the Galatians to return to the life in the Spirit that they had abandoned. Hence he writes not to the opponents but to the Galatians themselves,[5] hoping to restore them to the life of the Spirit. We may see his pastoral theology in the outcome that he proposes for his community.

Paul's Response to the Problem in Galatia

God's Children: Paul's Argument in 1:1–4:11

Paul's desire to win the Galatians determines the flow of the letter's argument. Galatians is not a forensic speech designed only to win the argument with the opponents; it has more the qualities of the deliberative speech, designed to persuade the listeners to adopt a specific course of action.[6] Therefore the imperatives that begin in 4:12 are not appendices to the argument but the

4. See W. Bauer, F. W. Danker, W. F. Arndt, and F. W. Gingrich, *Greek-English Lexicon of the New Testament and Other Early Christian Literature*, 3d ed. (Chicago: University of Chicago Press, 1999), 642. *Metatithēmi* is used in Greek literature for the "turncoat" who left the Stoics to become an Epicurean. In 2 Macc. 7:24 it is used when Antiochus encourages the young man to "turn away from the ways of his ancestors."

5. James D. G. Dunn, *The Theology of Paul's Epistle to the Galatians* (Cambridge: Cambridge University Press, 1993), 8.

6. George Kennedy, *New Testament Interpretation through Rhetorical Criticism* (Chapel Hill: University of North Carolina Press, 1984), 145. See also François Vouga, "Zur rhetorischen Gattung des Galaterbriefes," *Zeitschrift für die neutestamentliche*

culmination of the argument that Paul has been building from the beginning of the letter.[7] That is, Paul establishes the categories for discussion in the first four chapters and then draws out the implications in chapters 5 and 6 for the formation of the community.[8] In 1:10–2:14, as elsewhere in Pauline correspondence, he argues first from his personal ethos, introducing the major themes of the letter. This historical retrospective serves as the *narratio* for the argument to follow. In 1:10–24 he argues that the gospel the Galatians have deserted came to him directly by revelation (1:16), and he presents himself as a model of one who experienced a radical change from Judaism (1:13) to faith in Jesus Christ. The contrast between "formerly" (1:13–14) and "but when" (1:15) describes a decisive event demarcating the change in Paul's life and anticipates the description of the Galatians' conversion and relapse.[9] In 2:1–14 he presents a history of the case now confronting the Galatians, demonstrating that he took his stand for freedom (2:4–5) and the truth of the gospel against those who desired to enslave Gentile converts through the ritual requirements of Torah. In 2:15–21 his announcement of the theme of the letter functions as the *propositio* that he will argue. He introduces the subject of justification by faith (2:16) and describes himself as one who died to the law in order to live to God and be crucified with Christ (2:19–21). Thus he provides a model of the transformed existence that he wants the Galatians to imitate (4:12).

Paul develops the argument in 3:1–6:10, the *probatio* of the letter. The cumulative effect of the argument in chapters 3 and 4 is to reaffirm what Paul has declared in the salutation:

Wissenschaft 79 (1998): 291, for the parallels in arrangement between Galatians and Demosthenes' speech *De pace* (*Peri tēs eirēnēs*).

7. Frank J. Matera, "The Culmination of Paul's Argument to the Galatians: Gal. 5.1–6.17," *Journal for the Study of the New Testament* 32 (1987): 79.

8. The division of the argument in Galatians is notoriously difficult. As argued below, Galatians 5 is not a radical break in the argument, for Paul moves slowly from his direct argument to the Galatians and presents a sustained appeal beginning at 5:13. See below, p. 73.

9. George Lyons, *Pauline Autobiography: Toward a New Understanding,* Society of Biblical Literature Dissertation Series 73 (Atlanta: Scholars Press, 1985), 150.

that Christ has "set us free from the present evil age" (1:4). He establishes the identity of the Galatians as the adult children of Abraham (3:6–29), who can now address God as Father (4:1–6), and as the children of the free woman, Sarah (4:21–31). Thus he establishes a group identity for the Galatians, demonstrating that they do not need to heed the opponents' calls for the Jewish boundary markers in order to be children of God.[10] In the gift of the Spirit, the community has received the power of the new age (3:3–5). Paul assumes the apocalyptic distinction between the two ages when he divides history into the time "before faith came" (3:23) and the time when "faith has come" (3:25), declaring that the "fullness of time" has come (4:4). God sent his Son (4:4) to redeem those who were under the law (4:5) and to provide the promise of the Spirit (3:14), enabling the Gentile community to say, "Abba! Father" (4:6). In leaving "the present evil age" (1:4) to become children of God in the new age, the Galatians have exchanged slavery (4:8) for freedom. In a remarkable tour de force, Paul argues in 4:21–31 that the Gentile Christians are, in fact, the children of Sarah, the free woman (4:31). In this familial language, Paul reassures the Galatians of a corporate identity that does not depend on the acceptance of the deeds of Torah. This corporate identity is central to Paul's pastoral theology.

Paul's affirmation in chapters 3 and 4 that Christ has "set us free" is accompanied by two features that set the stage for chapters 5 and 6. In the first place, Paul speaks in antinomies that correspond to the distinction between the two ages.[11] He presents the antitheses of Christ and the law (2:19), Spirit and flesh (3:3), freedom and slavery (4:1–5, 8–11), faith and works (3:2, 6–14), and promise and law (3:15–18), arguing that "in Christ Jesus you are all children of God. . . . As many of you as were baptized"—including Gentile Christians—"have put on Christ" (3:26–27). In his claim that there is no longer Jew or

10. Philip Esler, "Group Boundaries and Intergroup Conflict in Galatians," in *Ethnicity and the Bible*, ed. Mark G. Brett (Leiden: Brill, 1996), 228.

11. See J. Louis Martyn, "Apocalyptic Antinomies in Paul's Letter to the Galatians," *New Testament Studies* 31 (1985): 415.

Greek, slave or free, male and female (3:28), Paul anticipates the closing paragraph of the letter, where he describes the "new creation" (6:15) in which Christians now live.[12] These antitheses refer to the narrative nature of the Galatians' corporate existence, suggesting that their conversion is only the beginning of God's work among them. Between the antitheses Paul accepts no middle ground. In the second place, because there is no middle ground, Paul speaks of the Galatians' relapse from one world to another—from faith to works, from Spirit to flesh, from freedom to slavery. They have turned to another gospel (1:6–9) and returned to the "weak and beggarly elemental spirits" (4:9) and "fallen from grace" (5:4). Indeed, he equates their turn to law as a relapse into the slavery to idolatry and to the "weak and beggarly elemental spirits" (4:8–10). Hence Paul says, "I fear that I have labored in vain" (4:11), indicating that their relapse reflects the failure of his pastoral work.

Until Christ Is Formed in You: Paul's Argument in 4:12–5:12

The words of 4:11, spoken in the context of the Galatians' relapse, present a different perspective from that expressed in 1 Thessalonians and Philippians, where Paul expresses the desire not to "run in vain" (Phil. 2:16; 1 Thess. 3:5). This plaintive expression marks an important transition in Paul's argument, for the imperative "Brothers [NRSV, 'friends'], become as I am" (4:12) is the first exhortation to the community. Scholars, accustomed to dividing Paul's letters between theological and ethical sections, have debated precisely where Paul moves from theology to ethics in Galatians. This distinction is misleading in Galatians, as the units in 4:12–19 and 5:1–12 begin with imperatives and continue with the theological argument of the letter. Thus these units form a bridge between the arguments of 1:10–4:11 and the sustained exhortation in 5:13–6:11. Paul looks to the future, exhort-

12. Ibid.

ing his readers to recall the early days of their conversion (4:12–20) and to stand in the freedom that they have gained in Christ (5:1, 13), in order to complete the narrative. We may therefore regard chapters 5 and 6 not as an appendix to the argument but as the logical conclusion to a letter in which Paul has described the powers of the new age that the community has already experienced. Having described the past events in 1:1–4:11—the Galatians' liberation and their relapse—he turns to the future in 4:12. After the transitional section in 4:12–5:12, where Paul speaks of both past and future, the final section in 5:13–6:10 holds out hope for the Galatians' ultimate transformation and offers instructions for maintaining the freedom that Paul describes in 3:1–4:11. This transformation is the conclusion to the narrative existence of the Galatians, which determines Paul's ministry.

The call to imitation, a frequent motif in Paul's letters (cf. 1 Cor. 11:1; Phil. 4:9), marks the beginning of Paul's attempt to restore the Galatians to their original status and to ensure that he did not "run in vain"—that is, that they complete their narrative. He looks to both the future and the past, addressing the Galatians as "brothers," recalling the community's founding (Gal. 4:12–16; cf. 1 Cor. 1:10–2:5; 1 Thess. 1:5–10) as a time of remarkable intimacy within the circle of a family. Now he asks where this blessedness has gone (Gal. 4:15). In his absence, the presence of the opposing teachers has undermined this intimacy and increased Paul's distress (4:17–18), as the remarkable metaphor of 4:19 indicates. Paul's appeal to them as his "children" (*tekna*) in 4:19 maintains the intimacy of 4:12–17 and recalls his parental images elsewhere where he speaks of himself as father (cf. 1 Cor. 4:14–15; 1 Thess. 2:12; Philem. 10) and even as "nurse" (1 Thess. 2:7) to his converts. The Galatians are his children because he is the founder of the community. In the words "for whom I am again in the pain of childbirth until Christ is formed in you" (Gal. 4:19 NRSV) Paul employs a maternal image, suggesting that he suffers the pains of childbirth as Christ, like an embryo, takes shape among the

Galatians.[13] Although the metaphor appears to be hopelessly
mixed, the passage echoes the occasions when Paul describes
his anxiety for the churches (cf. 2 Cor. 11:28) and continues
the expression of fear for his community in Galatians 4:11,
allowing him to speak both of his pain and of the church's
formation—themes that he develops elsewhere.

The imagery of the pain of childbirth echoes Old Testament
language according to which God is father and mother.
According to Isaiah 45:10, God is not only the potter working with the clay but the father who begets and the mother
who is in labor. According to Isaiah 66:7, before the pain of
labor, Israel bore a son.[14] Throughout the Old Testament and
apocalyptic literature, the people of God experience labor pains
before their ultimate deliverance.[15] Paul employs the imagery
of birth pangs in 1 Thessalonians 5:3, describing the anguish
that will precede the end. According to Romans 8:22, the whole
creation experiences birth pangs before the end. The maternal
image anticipates Paul's argument in Galatians 4:21–31, where
he appeals to the Isaiah passage to affirm that the church is
the child of the Spirit. Paul appeals to the apocalyptic image
of birth pangs to indicate that, despite the pain involved, the
people of God will live.

The birth pangs are not those of the community but of Paul
himself. Although he is already the parent to the Galatians,
his birth pangs have not ceased, for the Galatians have not yet
been formed. Paul's frequent references to his own sufferings
on behalf of the people illuminate this metaphor. The "sufferings of Christ overflow" in his own life (2 Cor. 1:5), as he
identifies himself with the crucified Christ and carries around
the dying of Jesus Christ in his own body (2 Cor. 4:10). In his

13. Frank J. Matera, *Galatians*, Sacra pagina 9 (Collegeville, MN: Liturgical Press,
1992), 166.

14. See G. Bertram, "*ōdin*," in *Theological Dictionary of the New Testament*, ed.
G. Kittel and G. Friedrich, trans. G. W. Bromiley, 10 vols. (Grand Rapids: Eerdmans,
1964–1976), 9:669.

15. Beverly Gaventa, "The Maternity of Paul," in *The Conversation Continues:
Studies in Paul and John in Honor of J. Louis Martyn*, ed. Robert T. Fortna and Beverly
R. Gaventa (Nashville: Abingdon, 1990), 193. Cf. Mic. 4:10; Isa. 13:6, 8; Jer. 6:24.

own ministry, Paul knows the "fellowship of his sufferings" (Phil. 3:10). Paul's statement that he has been "crucified with Christ" and that Christ now lives in him (Gal. 2:19) provides the context for our understanding of his birth pangs. As the founder of the church and participant in the work of God, he identifies with the eschatological birth pangs of the people of God and with the crucified Christ. Paul's mixed metaphor of being in birth pangs until Christ is formed among the Galatians reflects his total identification with Christ.

Paul's metaphor is so striking that interpreters easily lose sight of his larger point: that the Galatians' failures may not be permanent. The phrase "until Christ is formed in you" (4:19) signifies Paul's hope for the ultimate formation of the community despite the apparent failure. We may compare Paul's use of Greek words for "until" elsewhere to describe the formation of the church (cf. Phil. 1:6). The ultimate goal that Christ be formed among the Christians is the center of his pastoral theology. The language recalls Paul's understanding elsewhere that Christians are transformed by Christ. According to Philippians 3:10, Paul has been "conformed" to the cross of Christ. In 2 Corinthians 3:18, Paul affirms that the community is "being transformed" into Christ's image. In Romans 12:2 he encourages the community to be "transformed by the renewing of [their] mind." In each of these instances, the forms of *morph-* are in the passive voice, indicating that "the formation of Christ is a gift, not an achievement."[16] "Among you" is plural; although the modern reader thinks of this language in individualistic terms, Paul no doubt envisions Christ taking shape in the corporate community. What Paul desires is what he exemplifies: "Not I who live but Christ who lives in me" (Gal. 2:20)—that is, the crucified Christ.[17]

Paul's argument in 1:1–4:11 allows us to see how chapters 5 and 6 fit into the entire argument of Galatians. We need not conclude that Paul is fighting on two fronts—one that favors

16. Ibid., 197.
17. Witherington, *Grace in Galatia*, 315.

law keeping as a means to salvation (1:1–4:31) and one that is libertine in its outlook (5:1–6:10). Nor must we conclude that Paul faces a Jewish Gnosticism that combines law keeping with libertinism. In the apocalyptic antinomies that provide a thread running through Galatians, we see the unity of the letter. Paul has presented stark alternatives: Spirit or flesh, the new creation or the "present evil age" (1:4), freedom or slavery, faith or works of the law. The church cannot inhabit a middle ground between the two. After affirming that the community has received the power of the Spirit and that it has been liberated from slavery (1:1–4:12), Paul reaffirms this freedom (4:21–31) and challenges the community to recognize that the maintenance of this freedom requires the continuing presence of the Spirit. Paul's imperatives in 5:1, 13 introduce his instructions for living within the realm of the Spirit in order to maintain freedom and continue the formation described in 4:19.

In the words "For freedom Christ has set us free" (5:1) and "You were called to freedom" (5:13), Paul summarizes the argument of chapters 1–4. In the imperatives of 5:1, 13 he turns from the past to the future that he envisions if Christ is to be formed in them. In the call not to return to a yoke of slavery (5:1), he summarizes the argument against circumcision once more, indicating that one must choose between aeons. There is no middle ground, for "a little leaven leavens the whole lump" (5:9). In the parallel section that begins in 5:13, he warns against using freedom as an opportunity to return to the flesh. The fact that these two parallel passages appear to go in different directions—against a return to law in 5:1–2 and against apparent antinomianism in 5:13–26—does not reflect Paul's need to fight on two fronts or his anticipation of objections to his doctrine of justification by faith. In both instances, he is challenging the church to live within the new aeon, which is distinguished by freedom rather than slavery, Spirit rather than flesh. The abandonment of the Spirit in order to return to the flesh will result in the antisocial vices mentioned in 5:13–26, and the community will be torn apart by the self-seeking that is involved in the desire of the flesh. Freedom can exist only within the sphere of the Spirit (*pneuma*). Paul's linking of the antisocial vices with a return to the law may be a response to the opponents' claim that only by keeping the Torah could the Galatians maintain control of the desire of the flesh.

The imperative that begins in 5:13 offers instructions that will result in Christian formation. "Do not use your freedom as an opportunity for self-indulgence [literally, 'the flesh']" introduces his contrast between flesh and Spirit (5:16), continuing this dichotomy from 3:2 and 4:21–31. Paul challenges the Galatians to continue their lives just as they began: under the power of the Spirit (3:2–3).[18] As children of the Spirit (4:29) and of the free woman (4:31), they should not live within the sphere of the flesh, for freedom and flesh belong on opposite sides of the apocalyptic divide and result in antithetical modes of existence. In 5:13–15 Paul introduces these antithetical modes of existence before elaborating on them in 5:16–6:10. As the people who have been "rescued from the present evil age" (1:4), the Galatians face the choice between the two ages, that is, between Spirit and flesh.

The structure of the passage indicates the center of gravity of Paul's argument. In 5:13–26 we note a series of imperatives accompanied by explanatory comments. After the reaffirmation of the community's freedom in 5:13a, he says,

> Only do not use your freedom as an opportunity for self-indulgence, but through love become slaves to one another.
> For the whole law is fulfilled in a single commandment, "You shall love your neighbor as yourself."
> If, however, you bite and devour one another, take care that you are not consumed by one another.
> Live by the Spirit, I say, and you assuredly will not carry out the desires of the flesh.[19]

18. John M. G. Barclay, *Obeying the Truth* (Minneapolis: Fortress, 1988), 111.

19. Although *telesēte* can be an imperative, the context here is an assurance that the Galatians will overcome the destructive powers of the flesh. *Ou mē* with the subjunctive indicates the most definite form of negation about the future; F. Blass,

> For what the flesh desires is opposed by the Spirit . . .
> to prevent you from doing what you want.
> For the works of the flesh are obvious (v. 19). . . .
> By contrast, the fruit of the Spirit is love, joy,
> peace. . . .
> Those who belong to Christ have crucified the flesh
> and its desires (v. 24).
> If we live by the Spirit, let us also be guided by the
> Spirit.
> Let us not become conceited, competing against one
> another, envying one another.

The imperatives indicate that the Christians are faced by two major powers. Although they have abandoned the Spirit for the flesh (3:3), they nevertheless are free to choose between these two powers. The exhortation is Paul's plea for the Galatians to reaffirm the power of the new aeon in their lives. In the elaboration that accompanies each exhortation, Paul describes the consequences of living under both of the alternative powers. In 6:1–10 he addresses those who live in the new aeon to describe the community life that results from this existence.

Christian Formation as Care for Others in 5:13–6:10

The opening imperative, "Through love become slaves to one another" (5:13), is the heading for the entire section (5:13–6:10) and an elaboration of 5:6, according to which the only thing that matters is "faith working through love." This command introduces the theme of love and its alternative as Paul encourages the corporate identity that he established in Galatians 3

A. Debrunner, and R. W. Funk, *A Greek Grammar of the New Testament and Other Early Christian Literature* (Chicago: University of Chicago Press, 1961), 365. See Matera, *Galatians*, 199; J. Louis Martyn, *Galatians*, Anchor Bible 33A (New York: Doubleday, 1998), 65; Witherington, *Grace in Galatia*, 393. *Teleō* is often used for one who "keeps" or "fulfills" the commandments (cf. Rom. 2:27; James 2:8). Hence Paul's use of the verb for those who "gratify" (literally, "fulfill") the desire of the flesh may be a response to opponents who encourage the Galatians to "fulfill" the law; cf. Martyn, *Galatians*, 492.

and 4. In the Spirit, members turn from self-centeredness to become each other's slaves. Love leads the list of the fruit of the Spirit (5:22). In the word "one another" Paul anticipates the emphasis on others within the community. They bear one another's burdens (6:2), and they do good to all, especially those in the household of faith (6:10). Here, as in Romans 13:8, Paul transforms the Old Testament command for love of neighbor and indicates that the law is fulfilled by the realization of this love within the community. Having established that the Galatians are a family in chapters 3 and 4, he challenges them to live as family.[20] To the Galatians who have been attracted to the idea of fulfilling the law, Paul is saying that true fulfillment of the law occurs when believers deny themselves in order to look to the interests of others within the community. "If the Galatians really wanted to do the law—then they should stick to the *pneuma* and Christ!"[21]

Love for one another is shaped by the Christ who "loved me and gave himself for me" (cf. Gal. 2:20). The antithetical behavior is to bite and devour one another and thus to live within the sphere of the flesh. This description anticipates the antisocial vices in 5:19–21 and the concluding exhortation, "Let us not become conceited, competing against one another, envying one another" (5:26 NRSV).[22]

Paul's description of Christian formation is consistent with the goals he expresses for his churches in Philippians and 1 Thessalonians. The exhortation to become slaves to each other through love is parallel to his prayers for the communities of Philippi and Thessalonica to abound in love (Phil. 1:9–11; 1 Thess. 3:11–13). In Philippians, as in Galatians, Paul assumes that the community has a "consolation from love" and "sharing

20. Philip Esler, "Imagery and Identity in Gal 5:13–6:10," in *Constructing Early Christian Families*, ed. H. Moxnes (London: Routledge, 1997), 140.

21. Troels Engberg-Pedersen, *Paul and the Stoics* (Louisville: Westminster John Knox, 2000), 161.

22. Esler, "Imagery and Identity," 139, cites Plutarch, *De fraterno amore* (*Peri philadelphias*) 486B as a parallel to Paul's exhortation. Plutarch offers the hostility of wild animals toward one another in the search for food as conduct that brothers should avoid.

in the Spirit" (Phil. 2:1) forming the basis for his call for them to abandon self-seeking and to look to the interests of others. Paul consistently expresses the conviction that the community is transformed by the power of God.

"I say" (*legō de*) in Galatians 5:16, rendered more appropriately as "what I mean to say is this,"[23] indicates that the following section is an explanation of the promise that the Galatians will overcome the desire of the flesh that results in the hostility described in 5:15. In 5:16b this command is accompanied by a promise, rather than a restatement of the imperative as in "and do not gratify the desires of the flesh" (NRSV); the preferable translation of *kai epithymian sarkos ou mē telesēte* is, "You will assuredly not gratify the desire of the flesh." Although the desire of the flesh remains a genuine threat to Christian formation, Paul assures the Galatians that the power of the Spirit provides the means for the Christian to overcome such a desire. This confident assertion is analogous to the reassurance that he gives, in his other letters, of the continuing presence of divine power in the community of faith (Phil. 1:6; 1 Thess. 2:13).

His assurance of the capacity to overcome the problem of desire (*epithymia*) in Galatians 5:16, 24 addresses one of the fundamental concerns of ancient moralists.[24] Aristotle and the Stoics described the harmful effects of passion and offered suggestions for conquering it.[25] Hellenistic Jewish literature described the heroes who overcame *epithymia*[26] and attracted Gentiles with its claim that faithfulness to the Torah was the means of gaining self-mastery.[27] In numerous instances Paul speaks of *epithymia* in negative terms, associating it with the

23. Engberg-Pedersen, *Paul and the Stoics*, 162.

24. Dale Martin, "Paul without Passion," in *Constructing Early Christian Families*, ed. H. Moxnes (London: Routledge, 1997), 204–10.

25. Aristotle, *Ethica nichomachea* 7.1150b; Epictetus, *Diatribae (Dissertationes)* 2.16.45; 2.18.8. See F. Büchsel, "*epithumia*," in *Theological Dictionary*, ed. Kittel and Friedrich, 3:169.

26. See 4 Macc. 1:1–12.

27. See also Stanley Stowers, *A Rereading of Romans* (New Haven: Yale University Press, 1994), 64–65.

flesh (*sarx*, Rom. 13:14) or the body (*sōma*, Rom. 6:12). He regards *epithymia* as an alien power to which one may be enslaved (cf. Rom. 1:24–26; 6:12),[28] and he instructs new converts to avoid the "lustful passion" (*mē en pathei epithymias*) characteristic of the Gentiles (1 Thess. 4:5). Paul's assurance to the Galatians that the Spirit is the means to overcome the "desire of the flesh" is probably a response to the Galatians' attempt to gain control of the passions through the keeping of Torah.[29] The particular manifestation of the "desire of the flesh" that they will master is evident within the argument of Galatians 5:16–26. As the contrast to reciprocal love indicates (5:14–15), the "desire of the flesh" refers to the human who is driven by self-seeking.[30] Under the power of the flesh, they bite and devour each other (5:15). The "works of the flesh" in 5:19–21 include both offenses created by the libido and the anticommunal vices that Paul lists. These vices correspond to similar vices that Paul attributes elsewhere to the pre-Christian existence (cf. Rom. 1:18–32; 1 Cor. 6:9–11). Thus Paul promises in 5:16 that, under the power of the Spirit, members will no longer bite and devour each other. Those who belong to Christ will overcome the works of the flesh that manifest their lack of self-control. They will no longer find their identity in the pursuit of their own interests but will crucify the passions and lusts of the flesh. Christians are not defenseless in this battle between flesh and Spirit; they may choose between these two opposing forces. Thus in the imperatives of 5:16 and 5:25, Paul exhorts the believers to "walk by the Spirit" (5:16) and to "be guided by the Spirit" (5:25). They may choose between sowing to the flesh and sowing to the Spirit (6:8). As the structural analysis on pages 72–73 indicates, the dominant motif of the paraenetic section is the exhortation to reaffirm the Spirit in the context of

28. Klaus Berger, *Historische Psychologie des Neuen Testaments*, Stuttgarter Bibelstudien 146–147 (Stuttgart: Katholisches Bibelwerk, 1991), 165.

29. Stowers, *Rereading of Romans*, 72.

30. Hans Weder, "Normativität der Freiheit," in *Paulus, Apostel Jesu Christi*, ed. M. Trowitzsch (Tübingen: Mohr Siebeck, 1998), 140.

the opposition between flesh and Spirit (5:17), which make competing claims on the Christian's life.

This opposition between flesh and Spirit is not to be understood as an anthropological or ontological statement, for flesh and Spirit are the powers of the old and new aeons. For Paul, "Spirit" (*pneuma*) is not a quality inherent in the human but is the power of the new age that God has provided the believer (3:2–3, 14; 4:6). Flesh (*sarx*) belongs to the "present evil age" (1:4). It is the locus of natural human desire (5:16), which results in the "works of the flesh" (5:19–21). *Sarx* appears to refer to the human condition apart from the empowering effects of God's Spirit.[31] Paul's promise that the life of the Spirit empowers one to avoid the "desire of the flesh" is parallel to his statement in 5:24 that "those who belong to Christ Jesus have crucified the flesh with its passions and desires" (NRSV). In the two parallel passages, Paul offers an alternative to the life dominated by the flesh within a community that is empowered by the Spirit and has overcome the desires of the flesh.

This confident assertion requires explanation, for the experience of the Galatians demonstrates that Christian transformation is not inevitable. Despite the promise that they will not carry out the desire of the flesh, they continue to live within its domain. As Paul has already indicated, the Galatians have retreated from Spirit to flesh (3:3). Paul's assertion appears to deny the reality of the forces that undermine Christian transformation. If Paul's assertion in 5:16 is correct, one may reasonably ask why it appears to be unrealistic in actual experience. The description of people behaving as animals, biting and devouring one another (5:15), may refer to the real experience of the readers, who are not immune from the desire of the flesh. In 5:17, *gar* indicates that Paul will now explain the affirmation of 5:16.[32] The flesh "desires against" (or rises up in protest

31. See ibid., 134.
32. John J. Kilgallen, "The Strivings of the Flesh . . . (Galatians 5,17)," *Biblica* 80 (1999): 114.

against) the Spirit, and the Spirit against the flesh.[33] The two "are opposed" to each other, and Christians are caught in the middle. The result of this warfare is "to prevent you from doing what you want."[34]

Although Paul offers the description of the warfare between flesh and Spirit as an explanation for his promise that the Galatians will overcome the desire of the flesh, the meaning of the explanation in 5:17 is one of the most difficult exegetical problems in Galatians. If the passage indicates that the Christian is inevitably involved in a warfare between opposing powers, we cannot easily reconcile the explanation in 5:17 with the promise in 5:16. Furthermore, one may ask what Paul means by "doing what you want": is he describing the desires of the person under the control of the flesh or the desire to do good? To understand Paul's description of the warfare that prevents people from doing what they want, we must look at the entire argument in 5:13–6:10. Only after careful examination can we understand Paul's distinction between willing and doing in Galatians. Here the starting point for our understanding of Paul's portrayal of the divided existence is to observe, as above, that the imperative in 5:16 and the hortatory subjunctive in 5:25 frame the entire discussion in 5:16–26, elaborating on the alternatives posed in the introduction to the discussion in 5:13–15. The commands to "walk by the Spirit" (*pneumati peripateite*, 5:16) and "be guided by the Spirit" (*pneumati stoichōmen*, 5:25) imply that the Galatians have a choice between the two competing powers and that Paul challenges them to yield to the power that they have already received (3:3; 4:6). Despite the assurance in 5:16, the Galatians have not yet reached the goal that Paul enunciates in 5:16, 24. They have returned to the flesh (3:3), and they are probably engaged in biting and devouring one

---

33. On *epithymei*, see Bauer, Danker, Arndt, and Gingrich, *Greek-English Lexicon*, 372.

34. *Hina* here introduces a result clause: the result of the warfare, not its purpose.

another (5:15).[35] Consequently, the Galatians have not made the clear choice to "walk by the Spirit." They are caught in a warfare between flesh and Spirit, and they do not do what they want to do.

The distinction between willing and doing is an old one in philosophical and ethical literature.[36] Platonists and Stoics debated why humans do not do the good. Here and in Romans 7, Paul introduces a distinction between willing and doing. Although one should not read Romans 7:15 into Galatians 5:17, both passages describe the human attempt to do the good. To do what you want (Gal. 5:17) is to act ethically. The Galatians have turned to the law to gain self-control but have found themselves trying to live in both aeons. Although they have attempted to gain control over the flesh by keeping the Torah, they have failed. The result is that they bite and devour one another. Paul does not say, however, that this war is inevitable; nor is he describing the human condition in general. Rather, he is describing the result of living in both aeons. Those who have not clearly renounced the flesh are caught in this war. Those who live by the Spirit do not fulfill the desire of the flesh. Thus one may conclude here that Paul is not suggesting that Christians inevitably live with this struggle. Instead he is describing the fate of those who do not place themselves firmly in the domain of the Spirit. Indeed, according to 5:24, those who belong to Christ "have crucified the flesh with its passions and desires," following the example of Paul, who has been "crucified with Christ" (2:19).

The sharp dichotomy between flesh and Spirit is the background for Paul's affirmation "If you are led by the Spirit, you are not under law" (5:18). Law and flesh belong to the old aeon. Only under the Spirit will the community overcome the

35. J. Louis Martyn, "A Formula for Communal Discord as a Clue to the Nature of Pastoral Guidance," in *Putting Body and Soul Together*, ed. Virginia Wiles, Alexandra Brown, and Graydon F. Snyder (Valley Forge, PA: Trinity, 1997), 213.

36. Stowers, *Rereading of Romans*, 260–61.

desire of the flesh. Now there is no longer any need for the law to gain self-control.[37]

Whereas Paul says in Philippians that God empowers us "to will and to do" (2:13), here he speaks of the warfare that prevents people from doing what they will. Paul's consistent claim in Galatians of the Spirit's power to produce a transformed community, however, is consistent with his claim in Philippians. In Galatians, Paul insists that the community must choose this power if its will conforms to God's will. The description of the works of the flesh in Galatians 5:19–21 is an adaptation of a traditional ethical list that, no doubt, presents the portrait of those who have not come under the power of the Spirit. The Galatians, with their return to the flesh, may return to the "works of the flesh" mentioned in 5:19–21. Paul assumes that these belong to pre-Christian existence (cf. 1 Cor. 6:9–11), and he sees them as a potential threat for those who have put on Christ. The vices, in part, elaborate on the description in Galatians 5:15.

In keeping with his description of a community of love in 5:14, Paul describes the fruit of the Spirit as the consequence of living in the new aeon. "Love, joy, peace," and the other qualities mentioned are the fruit of living in the new aeon and the goal of Christian transformation. "Fruit" (*karpos*, 5:22) suggests that these qualities result from the empowerment of the Spirit. When "Christ is formed" (4:19) among the Galatians, the community will be distinguished by brotherly love and the associated qualities described as the fruit of the Spirit.[38] Christian formation consists in living under the power of the Spirit, which empowers the community to do the good.

In the imperatives of 6:1–10, Paul speaks to the community, offering illustrations of communal conduct that is antithetical to the life controlled by the flesh. In the first instruction, he assumes that the addressees are "spiritual" (*pneumatikoi*). They have responsibility to restore those who are caught in a

37. Engberg-Pedersen, *Paul and the Stoics*, 163.
38. Friedrich Wilhelm Horn, "Wandel im Geist," *Kerygma und Dogma* 38 (1992): 166.

trespass. Members of the community "bear one another's burdens, and fulfill the law of Christ" (6:2). The teachers and the other members of the community live in a reciprocal relation to each other (6:6). As a conclusion to the ethical section, Paul describes once more the choice facing the Galatians: they will sow either to the flesh or to the Spirit (6:7–8). Those who sow to the Spirit will continue to do the good to the "household of faith," the alternative family that Paul has described (6:9–10). Indeed, their good works will extend beyond the community "for the good of all."

Paul does not portray Christian existence as an inevitable struggle between opposing forces. Although the Galatian experience indicates that Christians may face this struggle if they attempt to live within both aeons, he encourages them that they can do the good (6:9) if they will submit to the power of the Spirit. As in Philippians and 1 Thessalonians, he envisions a church empowered to do the good. Despite the disappointments of pastoral ministry, Paul does not abandon hope, for he continues in birth pangs. He awaits their formation, and he offers instructions that will result in formation. Despite the complications in his relationship to the Galatians, he continues his pastoral ministry with them because his communal narrative with them is not finished. The hope for their transformation motivates his ministry.

A Final Word: The peroratio (6:11–18)

Paul's final words restate the argument of the letter with emotional force in a way that is characteristic of the *peroratio* of a speech. In 6:11–13 he again describes his opponents but in this instance questions their motives. As in the first two chapters, Paul presents himself as the alternative to the opponents and a model for the Galatians, recalling that he has been "crucified" (6:14; cf. 2:20) and that he bears the very marks of the crucified one (6:17). In his statement of the general principle that what matters is the "new creation" (6:15), he reiterates the letter's consistent claim that believers have been rescued "from the present evil age" (1:4) in order to live by the Spirit in the new aeon. This summary is the basis for a pastoral theology that is founded on the cross as the reality of the new age and the Spirit as the power for transformation.

The Pastoral Significance of Galatians

In Galatians, as in the other letters, we see the pathos of the minister concerned about the formation of the community. In contrast to Philippians and 1 Thessalonians, here this letter offers a glimpse of the messiness of pastoral ministry—of a work that is continually threatened. It depicts the pain of a pastoral ministry running the risk of being "in vain" even as it holds out the hope for the transformation of the community. Paul's goal for the community is analogous to the goal he expresses in his other letters. In the fruit of the Spirit, he speaks of an empowered community. The result will be a community empowered by the Spirit "through love" to "become slaves to one another." Paul's ultimate aim is to create a community that is shaped by the crucified Christ to abandon normal human self-seeking and look to the needs of others. In order to reach this goal, he offers specific instructions for the Christian life, challenging his converts to demonstrate the power of the Spirit through their corporate existence. His role as pastor is to offer a corporate ethical vision of a community that lives within the new creation.

Paul's pastoral vision is likely to be troubling for modern pastors. One wonders if Paul is realistic in his ambitions to shape a cruciform community by the power of God, especially in a culture of individualism that defines freedom as self-realization. We are more inclined to "accept our humanity" than to demand transformation into the image of the crucified and selfless Christ. Despite the hermeneutical difficulties of transferring Paul's pastoral vision into our own time, Paul's pastoral theology is helpful for contemporary practice. Although Paul does not concede that the Christian life is a perpetual struggle, he is not as unrealistic as some have suggested. He does not assume that this community experiences perfection; he recognizes that members of the community will be engaged in various trespasses (cf. 6:1). He argues, however, that the community of faith is empowered to care for and restore those who fall, keeping them within the sphere of the Spirit. Paul's emphasis on a communal narrative and corporate identity is a helpful contribution to the individualism of our own society. His focus on a new, extended family, the "household of faith" (6:10), can be a vital contribution to an urban culture in which many are uprooted from their own families. His claim that the community is the sphere in which we can do the good offers the potential for a corporate narrative in which the church is being transformed.

4

Romans as Pastoral Theology

Romans has played a significant role in pastoral theology, as discussed in chapter 1, above. Paul's declaration that "all . . . are now justified by his grace as a gift" (Rom. 3:23–24) is the foundation for an understanding of ministry that focuses primarily on the offer of acceptance to the individual. The fact that God accepts the unacceptable and forgives sinners has provided orientation to caregivers who have defined their work in terms of becoming channels of God's forgiveness, helping troubled people to accept themselves. Undoubtedly, Paul's word that "while we were yet sinners, Christ died for us" (5:8) has been a source of liberation for troubled people in modern times, just as it was for Luther. In the same way, Paul's anguished expression "I cannot do what I want" (7:15) has been the source of encouragement to people who assumed that Paul also struggled with temptation. Without questioning the importance of God's acceptance of the ungodly as an important insight for ministry, this chapter will show that Paul's pastoral theology is far more comprehensive than is often assumed. As recent scholarship has shown, the traditional reading ignores both the historical setting in which Paul writes and the place of Paul's doctrine of grace within the argument of the letter. Romans does contain a pastoral theology, but not one that is limited to God's acceptance of the individual. As the structure of the letter indicates, Paul's doctrine of justification by faith has profound implications for the moral life and community formation.

Although Romans is not, as earlier interpreters have maintained, a "compendium of Paul's theology," the length of the letter and the fact that Romans expands on some of the issues that Paul has treated in earlier letters suggest that this letter transcends the local situation to offer a theological perspective on the major issues that confronted Paul in all of his travels. "What makes Romans tick," according to Leander Keck, is the fact that "Paul did not allow his immediate situation to govern completely what he had to say, but allowed the inner logic of his gospel to assert itself even if that meant subjecting his first readers to a certain amount of theological overkill."[1] The letter lacks the intimate tones of some earlier letters (cf. Phil. 1:7–8; 1 Thess. 2:17–19; Gal. 4:19) and the combative tones of others (e.g., 2 Corinthians, Galatians). Writing to a church with which he has no prior relationship, Paul speaks both to a perceived local situation and to the broader context of his ministry. With its more comprehensive reflections, Romans provides a pastoral vision that encompasses Paul's entire mission, as he indicates at the conclusion of the letter (Rom. 15:14–30).

With its expansion of the themes from the earlier letters, Romans elaborates on the pastoral issues that we have seen in the preceding chapters of this book. In Romans he expands on the righteousness of God, a theme he introduces in Philippians (3:10) and 1 Corinthians (1:30) and develops in Galatians (3:6, 21; 5:5). We have seen that Paul has addressed the concern over willing and doing in Philippians 2:13 and Galatians 5:17. In Romans 7:7–25 Paul gives an extended treatment of this

1. Leander Keck, "What Makes Romans Tick?" in *Pauline Theology*, ed. Jouette M. Bassler, David M. Hay, and E. Elizabeth Johnson, 4 vols. (Minneapolis: Fortress, 1991–1997), 3:29.

problem. Indeed, Romans 5–8 appears to be an expansion of Galatians 4–6 as Paul elaborates on Christian experience and the challenges to the formation of the community. In Galatians (4:19) Paul refers to the formation of the community, anticipating the larger thematic statement in Romans 8:18–39 (esp. 8:29). He describes the struggle between flesh and Spirit and the challenge of overcoming "desire" (*epithymia*) in Galatians 5:1–6:10 before expanding on these themes in Romans 5–8. In Galatians Paul presents an unholy alliance between the law and sin (Gal. 5:18, 23) and later develops this theme in Romans (7:7).[2] In Galatians (5:6) he describes Christian existence as waiting for the righteousness of God (cf. Phil. 3:20), and in Romans he describes both creation and believers as waiting for the renewal of the creation (8:19, 23). Thus Paul presents a comprehensive view of Christian existence, a view that is central for our understanding of his pastoral vision.

The Pastoral Situation and Purpose of Romans

In Romans Paul's argument transcends the local situation in two ways. In the first place, the fact that he never refers explicitly to the conditions of the Roman church may suggest that he does not know the Roman situation in detail. All our reconstructions of the Roman situation depend on the mirror reading of the content of this letter, external evidence about Roman Christianity, and the evidence provided by Romans 16.[3] From the evidence of the letter, we know only that the readers are predominantly Gentiles (1:6, 13; 11:13) and that Paul has never visited them. The list of names in chapter 16 indicates

2. Troels Engberg-Pedersen, "Galatians in Romans 5–8 and Paul's Construction of the Identity of Christ Believers," in *Texts and Contexts*, ed. Tord Fornberg and David Hellholm (Oslo: Scandinavian University Press, 1995), 488.

3. See Robert J. Karris, "Romans 14:1–15:13 and the Occasion of Romans"; Wolfgang Wiefel, "The Jewish Community in Ancient Rome and the Origins of Roman Christianity"; Karl Paul Donfried, "False Presuppositions in the Study of Romans"; and Peter Lampe, "The Roman Christians of Romans 16," all in *The Romans Debate*, ed. Karl P. Donfried (Peabody, MA: Hendrickson, 1991).

a Jewish presence in the Roman church alongside the Gentile members. We may conclude therefore that Paul at least was aware of the demographics of a church composed of a majority of Gentiles with a significant Jewish presence. Indeed, arguments based on external evidence that Paul is addressing the tensions between Jewish and Gentile house churches after the relaxation of the edict of Claudius remain a possibility, though not conclusive.

In the second place, Paul writes at a turning point in his career, reflecting on his relationship not only to this community but to all of the churches he has founded (15:22–29). Thus Paul tells more about his own situation in the letter than about the Roman church. Having preached to Gentiles throughout the eastern Mediterranean world, he focuses on one major issue before he travels to Rome: the place of the Gentiles among the people of God and the ultimate success of his life's work as minister to the Gentiles (cf. 15:22–33). He will receive the ultimate test when he travels to Jerusalem to deliver the collection from the Gentile churches (15:25–28). He asks for the prayers of the Roman church (15:30–33) because he is unsure of the outcome of his Jerusalem visit. Not only is he concerned about the response of the "disobedient in Judea"; he is unsure that the saints will receive the offering (15:31). Thus, although Paul may not know the Roman situation in detail, he can assume that the issues that he faces everywhere are also present in Rome.

Although Paul may have more than one purpose in writing to the Romans, these aims fit within a more comprehensive goal of the apostle. He writes to persuade his readers to accept his own theological vision and to place them within a grand narrative in which Paul plays the decisive role. If we observe the interplay between the frame of the letter (1:1–17; 15:14–16:27), with its autobiographical reflections, and the argument of the letter (1:18–15:13), we see Paul's articulation of both his place and that of the Roman Christians in God's grand narrative.[4]

4. See Jeffrey A. Crafton, "Paul's Rhetorical Vision and the Purpose of Romans: Toward a New Understanding," *Novum Testamentum* 32 (1990): 332: "In Romans, Paul reconstitutes his apostleship, creating a persona which lives and functions and is

Romans is, as Nils Dahl observed, a missionary document.[5] It functions also, as Krister Stendahl argued, as a "final account" of Paul's theology of mission.[6] It is not, however, a mere accounting of why Jews and Gentiles get into a relationship with God. It is a challenge to the Roman church to accept the implications of Paul's theology of mission for its continuing life and transformation. Paul's pastoral vision is evident in his exploration of the full implications of the righteousness of God in the life of the church.

Paul's Pastoral Vision in the Frame of the Letter (1:1–17; 15:14–16:27)

At the beginning of Romans, Paul identifies his role in the grand narrative. He has been set apart for the gospel of God, which "he promised beforehand through his prophets" (1:2) concerning the Son, Jesus Christ. Paul has "received grace and apostleship for the obedience of faith among all the Gentiles . . . , including yourselves who are called to belong to Jesus Christ" (1:5). He connects his own mission with the summary of his gospel (1:3–6) and with the work of bringing the Gentiles into Israel's story. At the end of the letter, Paul expresses the same pastoral ambition for the "obedience of the Gentiles" (15:18; 16:19, 26), which includes both their initial acceptance of the message and their continued Christian existence (6:16, 17; 10:10).[7] Thus both he and the readers participate in a narrative

---

defined by the larger rhetorical vision. Paul describes his mission in terms of the realization of the promise of the Scriptures (1:1–2), the goal of which is to bring about the obedience of faith among all the nations (1:5; 15:18; 16:26), to reap a harvest among the nations (1:13), to present the nations as an offering to God (15:16)."

5. Nils Dahl, *Studies in Paul: Theology for the Early Christian Mission* (Minneapolis: Augsburg, 1977).

6. Krister Stendahl, *Final Account: Paul's Letter to the Romans* (Philadelphia: Fortress, 1995), ix.

7. Inasmuch as the opening words (1:1–13) introduce the subject of the letter and make the audience favorably disposed to the message, they function as the *exordium*. The repetition of the major themes in 15:14–30 and Paul's emotional appeal (15:29–30) give this section the quality of a *peroratio*.

of Israel's story that has now reached its culmination. In his role as apostolic emissary, Paul has wanted to come to Rome many times to "share with you some spiritual gift to strengthen you" (1:11) and to "reap some harvest among you as I have among the rest of the Gentiles" (1:13 NRSV). Despite the later claim that he preaches where Christ has not been named lest he build on another's foundation (15:26), Paul's aim in Rome is to engage in community formation, knowing that the church is an unfinished work. To "strengthen" (*stērichthēnai*, 1:11–12) is to sustain and to provide stability for the community, a task in which Paul and his emissaries engage (cf. 1 Thess. 3:2) but that ultimately is the work of God (1 Thess. 3:13).[8] To "reap a harvest" (*karpon echō*, literally "have fruit," Rom. 1:13) is also to contribute to the moral formation of the community, which once "bore fruit to death" (7:5) but is now able to "bear fruit to God" (7:4; cf. 6:19). Thus Paul hopes that a visit will contribute to the Romans' capacity to live out the consequences of the gospel.

That Romans, like Paul's other letters, is a substitute for his presence is especially evident in 1:14–17, where he continues to describe the reasons for his desire to come to Rome. Because of his desire to "have fruit" among the Romans and his indebtedness to Greeks and barbarians (1:14), he wants to preach (*euangelisasthai*) in Rome. The reference to his activity of preaching (*euangelisasthai*) leads him to clarify what the content of his gospel (*euangelion*) is[9] and to introduce the *propositio*, which indicates the case that Paul will argue: the gospel is the "power of God for salvation to everyone who has faith" because in it "the righteousness of God has been revealed" (1:16–17). That is, in the letter itself, Paul preaches the gospel, anticipating what he will do when he comes to Rome.[10] The claim that the gospel is "for everyone

8. See C. Spicq, *Theological Lexicon of the New Testament*, 3 vols. (Peabody, MA: Hendrickson, 1994), 3:292.

9. Neil Elliott, *The Rhetoric of Romans: Argumentative Constraint and Strategy and Paul's Dialogue with Judaism* (Sheffield, Eng.: JSOT Press, 1990), 82.

10. Ibid., 84.

who has faith" lays the basis for the argument of the letter, which focuses on the equal standing of Jews and Gentiles before God. The letter is thus a means of strengthening the congregation.

After making the argument in 1:18–15:13, Paul recapitulates the substance of 1:1–17 in 15:14–33, again describing his pastoral role and the Gentile community's place within God's grand narrative in terms that indicate Paul's pastoral vision. He concludes, "I have written to you rather boldly by way of reminder, because of the grace given me by God to be a minister [*leitourgos*] of Christ Jesus to the Gentiles in the priestly service of the gospel of God" (15:15–16 NRSV). His claim for a special commission to preach to the Gentiles recalls 1:6, 7. Thus the body of the letter (1:18–15:13) is a reminder of the gospel and an explanation of Paul's mission work. As a priest, he aims to present "the offering of the Gentiles . . . sanctified by the Holy Spirit" (15:16).[11] The offering of the Gentiles consists of the Gentiles themselves.[12] The offering of a sanctified community recalls his earlier calls for sanctification (6:18) and his prayer that the Thessalonians be strengthened "in holiness" (*en hagiōsynē*, 1 Thess. 3:13; cf. 5:23) and be blameless at the coming of Christ. Paul assumes that believers have been sanctified already (cf. 1 Cor. 1:2, 6:11), but he envisions sanctification as a continuing reality until the end. Thus the offering of the Gentiles is an eschatological act, the aim of Paul's entire ministry. Paul's work is not only to evangelize but to participate in the transformation of the community. The offering will not be "sanctified by the Holy Spirit" until Paul has completed his task.

This pastoral vision corresponds to Paul's statements in the other letters about the ultimate goal of his ministry. To offer

11. *Leitourgos* is the term used in the Septuagint for Levitical priests in a fixed cultic sense (cf. Exod. 28:35; Num. 8:22) and in Heb. 8:2 for the priestly work of Christ. Paul uses the term for the ministry of Epaphroditus in Phil. 2:25 and describes his own ministry as a *leitourgia* in Phil. 2:17.

12. Joseph Fitzmyer, *Romans: A New Translation with Introduction and Commentary*, Anchor Bible 33 (New York: Doubleday, 1992), 712.

the Gentiles as a sacrifice, according to Romans, is his "reason to boast" (*kauchēsis*, 15:17). Similarly, Paul claims elsewhere that his churches are his "boast" (2 Cor. 1:14; cf. 7:4; Phil. 2:16; 1 Thess. 2:19) at the coming of Christ. According to 2 Corinthians 11:2, he will "present" the church as a pure virgin to Christ at the end. Paul's pastoral ambition is to ensure that his churches are sanctified and blameless until the coming of Christ.

Paul's Pastoral Vision in the Body of the Letter: 1:18–15:13

1:18–4:25

If the body of Romans is the "reminder" (15:15) of Paul's mission and the basis for Paul's desire to present a sanctified community to God at the end, it is intended not only to justify the evangelization of the Gentiles but to persuade the Christians of Rome to live out the consequences of the gospel so that Paul may present them as an offering to God. Paul's argument is intended to strengthen (1:11) the community and contribute to its sanctification (15:16). Thus we notice the pastoral dimension of the entire argument.[13] The ultimate aim of Paul's ministry, as the closing words of the body of the letter indicate, is to present to God a community that "lives in harmony with one another" (15:5) and is able "with one voice to glorify God" (15:6).

Paul lays the foundation for his appeal to the Romans in the letter's *propositio* in 1:16–17 and the subsequent argument in 1:18–4:25, describing the new situation in God's narrative that has come with the Christ event. Although Paul shares with the Jewish tradition the expectation of a future judgment when God will vindicate the faithful and punish the wicked according to God's "righteous judgment" (2:5), the parallel

13. Troels Engberg-Pedersen, *Paul and the Stoics* (Louisville: Westminster John Knox, 2000), 183.

clauses "the righteousness of God is revealed" (*dikaiosynē* . . . *theou* . . . *apokalyptetai*, 1:17) and "the wrath of God is revealed" (*apokalyptetai* . . . *orgē theou*, 1:18) indicate that this judgment is a present reality. Paul employs apocalyptic language to indicate the eschatological situation that has already occurred, elaborating on this new situation in 3:21, when he says, "But now the righteousness of God has been disclosed," and in 3:26, when he speaks of the demonstration of God's righteousness "at the present time."[14] This "now" is the culmination of the narrative of God. Although Paul speaks of both wrath and righteousness as moments yet to come (cf. 2:5, 13), here he points to the present moment as the experience of both God's wrath and God's righteousness. God's wrath is revealed upon all disobedience, and both Jew and Gentile are under the power of sin (3:9). Similarly, God's righteousness is revealed for all who believe (1:17; 3:21–26). Thus God is impartial, and both Jew and Gentile stand equally before God.

According to 1:18–3:20, they stand equally under God's wrath. The paraenetic significance of this section is evident in its anticipation of the exhortations in 6:1–8:13 and its correspondence to 12:1–15:13. Whereas the latter two passages encourage the transformed existence (12:2), 1:18–3:20 describes humanity under the power of sin. Paul begins the argument with a description of those who do not do the will of God (1:18–3:20) and completes the argument with a depiction of life under the righteousness of God, a life in which believers do the will of God (12:2). Thus 1:18–3:20 is implicitly a description of the readers' past experience (cf. 6:17–22). The major focus of 1:18–3:20 is that humans, whether they observe the law or not, stand under God's wrath because they do not do the good that they know. In the opening line, Paul says that God's wrath is revealed against all "wickedness of those who by their wickedness suppress the truth" (1:18). Although they

---

14. Paul uses *apokalyptō* for the future eschatological event in Rom. 8:18; 1 Cor. 3:13; Phil. 3:15. He speaks of the present revelation in 1 Cor. 2:10.

know God through the evidence of nature (1:21), they do not act in accordance with God's will. Those who do not know the law exchange the truth for a lie (1:25); they "know God's decree . . . yet they not only do them but even applaud others who practice them" (1:32 NRSV).

The evidence of human unrighteousness (*adikia*) in 1:18–32 is the corruption of both mind and body. We note Paul's language of cognition not only in his description of the people's failure to act on what they know but also in his references to the distortions in their minds. They "became futile in their thinking, and their senseless minds were darkened" (1:21 NRSV). Pretending to be wise, "they became fools" (1:22). Hence "God gave them up to a debased mind [*nous*]" (1:28). This debasement of mind results in their enslavement to the passions. God likewise "gave them up in the lusts of their hearts to impurity, to the degrading of their bodies among themselves" (1:24 NRSV). Paul describes the conduct in 1:24–27 that constitutes the life enslaved to *epithymia*. The offenses that Paul describes entail enslavement to the passions, as evidenced in the homosexual acts described in 1:26–28 and the antisocial vices that he describes in 1:29–32.

Similarly, those who judge (2:1) also know God but fail to keep the law that they know (2:1–11, 17–24). Consequently, all who do not do the good are under the power of sin and subject to the wrath of God. The distinguishing feature of the community's past is self-centeredness; they disobey because of "self-seeking" (*eritheia*, 2:8)[15] just as those who know God only from nature are absorbed by enslavement to their own passions. Indeed, Paul says in 7:5 that even those who keep the law were overcome by passions of the flesh. This indictment, with its description of the enslavement of the passions and self-seeking, is implicitly a description of the initial stage of the community's own narrative, for the readers were once enslaved to sin (6:17), presenting their members to uncleanness

---

15. Engberg-Pedersen, *Paul and the Stoics*, 12.

(6:19, 20). Human transformation will require the conquering of these destructive passions.

In 2:12–16 Paul anticipates the argument that he will present in the concluding chapters. Having established the impartiality of God (2:11), Paul indicates that all who sin—with or without the law—stand under God's judgment (2:12), and he concludes, "For it is not the hearers of the law who are righteous in God's sight, but the doers of the law who will be justified" (2:13 NRSV). These doers of the law include Gentiles who do not keep the Torah in the same way that Jews do (2:14–16), for they have the law written on their hearts (2:15; cf. Jer. 31:33). Although the passage appears to contradict Paul's major argument for justification by faith in the remainder of the letter, it is not, as Sanders has argued, in contradiction to Paul's argument but a general statement that fits well with the claim that all stand on the same ground at the judgment.[16] At this point, Paul's statement is a general principle to which he appeals because it is a commonplace in Jewish literature.[17] He assumes that his interlocutor will agree.[18] In the present situation, however, Paul assumes that no one is a doer of the law, for "all . . . are under the power of sin" (3:9).[19] The general principle still stands, however, for, among those who no longer live in this age (cf. 12:1–2), a new people fulfill the law of God (8:4), not in the way that

16. E. P. Sanders, *Paul, the Law, and the Jewish People* (Philadelphia: Fortress, 1985), 123. "I think that in 1:18–2:29 Paul takes over to an unusual degree homiletical material from Diaspora Judaism, that he alters it in only insubstantial ways, and that consequently the treatment of the law in chapter 2 cannot be harmonized with any of the diverse things which Paul says about the law elsewhere. . . . Nevertheless 2:12–15 and 2:26 do not square well with the conclusion that all are under the power of sin (3:9, 20)" (pp. 123–24).

17. Klyne Snodgrass, "Justification by Grace—to the Doers: An Analysis of the Place of Romans 2 in the Theology of Paul," *New Testament Studies* 32 (1986): 77–79.

18. Richard Longenecker, "The Focus of Romans," in *Romans and the People of God*, ed. Sven Soderland and N. T. Wright (Grand Rapids: Eerdmans, 1999), 57.

19. See John W. Martens, "Romans 2.14–16: A Stoic Reading," *Theological Studies* 40 (1994): 63. In 2:14, the phrase "when the Gentiles . . . do what the law requires" is indefinite, suggesting the possibility that such a case might be found but not that it has been found.

Jews traditionally define it but in the way that Paul defines it in Romans (cf. 13:8–10).[20] Paul's goal is to guide the community toward this new existence. At the end "we will all stand before the judgment seat of God" (14:10), and "each of us will be accountable to God" (14:12).[21] Then "the doers of the law will be justified" (2:13).

Paul's address to the one who calls himself a Jew (2:17–24) also anticipates the later argument and reinforces the idea that no one presently meets the requirements for ultimate vindication. Like those who do not know the law (1:18–32), the interlocutor has been instructed in the law and thus "knows the will [of God] and determines what is best" (*ginōskeis to thelēma kai dokimazeis ta diapheronta*, 2:18), but does not live up to this standard (2:17–24). This charge anticipates Paul's appeal to the listeners to "discern the will of God [*dokimazein ti to thelēma tou theou*], the good and acceptable and perfect" (12:2). Similarly, according to Philippians 1:10, the transformed community will "determine what is best" (see p. 43). Paul adapts the Stoic distinction between the "things that are indifferent" (*ta adiaphora*) and the "better things" (*ta diapheronta*) to his own understanding of ethical progress in anticipation of the ethical vision that he presents in the letter.[22]

In 3:21–4:25 Paul argues that God's righteousness, like his wrath (1:18–3:20), is revealed to all peoples, overcoming the power of sin (3:21–22). In the death of Christ, God has demonstrated his righteousness (3:21, 25–26). Here Paul stacks up the words for the death of Christ as he associates God's righteousness with grace (*charis*), redemption (*apolytrōsis*), and sacrifice of atonement (*hilastērion*). Although God's righ-

---

20. See N. T. Wright, "The Law in Romans 2," in *Paul and the Mosaic Law*, ed. James D. G. Dunn (Grand Rapids: Eerdmans, 1996), 146–47.

21. See Snodgrass, "Justification by Grace," 74.

22. *Ta diapheronta* designates "what really matters"; W. Bauer, F. W. Danker, W. F. Arndt, and F. W. Gingrich, *Greek-English Lexicon of the New Testament and Other Early Christian Literature*, 3d ed. (Chicago: University of Chicago Press, 1999), 238.

teousness includes the forgiveness of the sinner and getting into a relationship with God, it includes significantly more, as the remainder of Romans will demonstrate. God's righteousness is, as Isaiah 40–66 indicates, an act of creation and restoration.[23] Those who are justified enter a new creation with the new possibility that they may "become the righteousness of God" (2 Cor. 5:21) and slaves of righteousness (Rom. 6:16). Believers have been justified (5:1) and still await the judgment when those who remain faithful "will be justified" (2:13). Thus God's righteousness is both an event and a continuing process that cannot be separated sharply from sanctification.[24] Just as all stand under God's wrath, both Jews and Gentiles stand not on the basis of ethnic privilege but on God's impartial righteousness, the fulfillment of Israel's narrative. According to Romans 4, Abraham is the father of many nations and the example of justifying faith. Indeed, the narrative of humanity in 3:21–22 ("all") becomes the community's narrative in 4:23–25, when Paul makes the transition to the first person plural to say that the believing community composed primarily of Gentiles has, like Abraham, believed in the one who raised Christ from the dead.

Paul's pastoral theology in Romans includes not only acceptance of the sinner but the reclamation of the sinner to a faithful life. Justification is not the answer to the individual's struggle with guilt but the loving compassion of God that transforms sinners and prepares them for ultimate vindication. In Romans 1–4 Paul speaks in the past (aorist and perfect) tenses to declare the good news that has created the community of believers. In the cross of Christ God has overcome sin.

23. Peter Stuhlmacher, *Revisiting Paul's Doctrine of Justification* (Downers Grove, IL: InterVarsity, 2001), 45.

24. Ibid., 67. "The controversial and—between Protestants and Catholics since the sixteenth century—much discussed distinction between "imputed" righteousness (which is only credited to the sinner [the Protestant view]) and "effective" righteousness (which transforms the sinner in his or her being [the Catholic view]) cannot be maintained from the Pauline texts. Both belong together" (p. 62).

5:1–8:39

Interpreters have frequently regarded Romans 1–4 as the heart of the letter.[25] More recent scholars, however, correctly note that these chapters in fact lay the foundation for Paul's argument in the remainder of Romans. The opening words of chapter 5, "Since we are justified by faith" (*dikaiōthentes oun ek pisteōs*), indicate that Paul builds on the past event described in chapters 1–4 to describe the community's continuing narrative. The distinguishing feature of this section is the first-person plural, which signifies the believing community, predominantly Gentile. Unlike chapters 1–4, with its focus on the past event, chapters 5–8 describe the full panorama of the community's story and its place in God's grand narrative. Chapter 5, with its reference to past and future, provides a rhetorical bridge between chapters 1–4 and 6–8.[26] In 5:1–11 Paul recalls the past event (5:1, 6–8) of Christ's saving death "for us" as the basis for the community's hope in the future. In the contrast between Adam and Christ in 5:12–21, Paul elaborates on the sinfulness of humanity discussed in 1:18–3:20 and anticipates the claim in chapter 6 that Christians have both died to sin and been incorporated into Christ within a new creation. Through the Holy Spirit, which God has granted to the church through the Christ event (5:5), the church now lives in hope, as Paul argues in chapter 8. Thus in chapters 5–8 Paul draws the consequences of the Christ event for the community's place in God's grand narrative of the world, indicating that the church stands in the middle of a story that is not yet complete.

5:1–11; 8:14–39

In the first (5:1–11) and final (8:14–39) sections, Paul places the believing community within God's grand narrative, arguing that the Christ event guarantees the future. Those who have

25. Longenecker, "Focus of Romans," 59.
26. Patricia M. McDonald, "Romans 5:1–11 as a Rhetorical Bridge," *Journal for the Study of the New Testament* 40 (1990): 81–96; Engberg-Pedersen, "Galatians in Romans 5–8," 480.

been justified will "be saved through him from the wrath of God" (5:9) and "will be saved by his life" (5:10). Because of the Christ event, the community lives in hope (5:2, 4–5), for it was "saved in hope" (8:24), but it now waits in patience (8:25), knowing that all things work for the ultimate good (8:28) for those who have been called. In a series of verbs in the aorist tense, Paul reaffirms the place of this Gentile community in God's grand narrative. Insofar as they are the ones whom God "foreknew," "predestined," "called," "justified," and "glorified," they have a place in God's plan from the beginning and have been vindicated in the Christ event (8:29–30). That their place in God's narrative is unfinished is evident in Paul's claim that "whom he foreknew he also predestined to be conformed to the image of his Son" (8:29). Thus, on the basis of God's saving acts in the past, the community expects transformation into the image of the resurrected Lord as the ultimate goal of the grand narrative. Paul's pastoral aim therefore is to present to God a new humanity composed of those who bear the image of Christ.[27]

The nature of this transformation is evident within the context of Romans 5–8. The transformation indicates what Paul means with the phrase "We shall be saved" (5:9). Paul anticipates the occasion when those who suffer with Christ "may also be glorified with him" (8:17). When Paul speaks of the liberation of creation and the liberation of our body (8:23), he looks beyond the immediate time to the ultimate transformation. Paul anticipates the redemption of both creation and the believing community. This transformation has not yet occurred; hence the community waits in hope.

Paul's description of this transformation is analogous to his consistent claim that the ultimate goal of his work is the transformation of believers into the image of Christ. In 1 Corinthians 15:49, he speaks of the resurrection body: "Just as we have borne the image of the man of dust, we will also bear the image

---

27. See L. Ann Jervis, "Becoming Like God through Christ: Discipleship in Romans," in *Patterns of Discipleship in the New Testament*, ed. Richard N. Longenecker (Grand Rapids: Eerdmans, 1996), 154.

of the man of heaven" (NRSV). According to 2 Corinthians 3:18, "we are being transformed into his image." We have seen in Philippians that Paul anticipates the time when "he will transform the body of our humiliation that it may be conformed to the body of his glory, by the power that also enables him to make all things subject to himself" (Phil. 3:21 NRSV). Paul's gospel therefore entails the total transformation of believers in a new creation. The offering of the Gentiles will be a transformed community.

In the meantime, the community waits with the whole creation (Rom. 8:19, 23) in the context of "the sufferings of this present time" (8:18; cf. 5:3). The reference to hardship, distress, persecution, famine, nakedness, peril, and sword (8:35) as well as death, life, angels, rulers, things present, things to come, and powers (8:38–39) indicates that the community still lives in the context of threatening forces. Thus God's narrative remains unfinished. Just as the creation lives in the bondage of decay, members of the community still live in anticipation of the redemption of the body, awaiting the eschatological transformation of creation and of their existence.

6:1–8:13

The beginning (5:1–11) and ending (8:14–39) units describe the community's place within God's grand narrative and ensure the ultimate transformation of creation and the community despite threatening forces. Because the community lives before the "redemption of the body" (8:23), the community's transformation requires the overcoming of the bodily passions that Paul described in 1:18–32. Paul points the way toward solving the problems he raised in 1:18–3:20, indicating that those who do the good that they know are the ones whom he will ultimately present as a sacrifice to God. In this section Paul speaks directly to the listeners, addressing them in the indicative (6:1–11, 14–18, 23; 7:1–8:14) to describe the new reality in which they live and in the imperative (6:12–13, 19) to instruct them to do the good. As he answers the questions of the interlocutor (6:1, 15; 7:7), he demonstrates how believers leave behind the existence described in 1:18–3:20 in order to be transformed. The obedience of the Gentiles, for which Paul has been commissioned (1:5), is not a matter of getting into a relationship with God but of a continuing transformation. Having demonstrated that "all are under the power of sin" (3:9), Paul now has the challenge of demonstrating how a community that still lives before the "redemption of the body" (8:23) can do the good, for the body is the locus of destructive and enslaving passions (*epithymiai*; cf. 6:12). Indeed, neither those who do not keep the law nor those who keep the law have been able to overcome *epithymiai* (cf. 1:24; 7:5). The twofold question in 6:1, 15 ("Should we continue in sin . . . ?" "Should we sin . . . ?") is the foil for Paul's argument that believers can indeed do the will of God apart from the works of Torah.

6:1–23. In 6:1–23 Paul answers the twofold question (6:1, 15) with parallel arguments that describe the nature of Christian transformation. In each instance, he answers the question first by appealing to what the believers already know (6:2, 16) about the event that constitutes the defining point in their corporate narrative—their death to sin and new existence in Christ. And in each instance, Paul's description of the new existence is followed by the imperative (6:12–13, 19), instructing them to do the good. In each case, Paul reminds the listeners of their own corporate narrative in order to give the basis for the imperative. That is, the new reality creates the basis for Christians to overcome the power of sin.

In recalling this defining event, Paul speaks not of their faith, as one might expect (cf. 4:25; 5:1), but of their baptism, which marks the boundary between the old and the new existence (6:4). In baptism, the story of Christ becomes the community's story as Paul adapts the early Christian confession (cf. 1 Cor. 15:3) to the listeners, who have participated in the death, burial, and resurrection of Christ.[28] Although the experience undoubtedly refers to individual listeners, it also describes the corporate

28. Paul does not actually say that Christians have been raised in Christ (cf. Col. 2:12), but he speaks of "newness of life" determined by the resurrection.

identity of believers, for the entire community shares the fate of
Christ.[29] The focus of Romans 6:1–11, as the *inclusio* in 6:2, 11
indicates, is the community's death to the old existence, which
is the prerequisite for "newness of life" (6:4). Paul's description
of this "newness" (*kainotēs*) presupposes the distinction between
the old and the new creation and assumes the community's
role in a cosmic narrative. In contrast to the old humanity in
which sin reigned (5:12–21), Christ is the founder of the new
humanity in which sin has lost its power. In the new covenant
of Jeremiah (31:31–34), believers indeed keep God's commands.
Just as Christ died and was buried, "we died to sin" (6:2) and
"were buried with him" (6:4). Christians therefore share the
fate of the founder of the new humanity. Just as his death was
"once for all" (6:10), the community shares "the likeness of
his death" (6:5). In this death, "our old self was crucified with
him so that the body of sin might be destroyed" (6:6). Just as
the death of Jesus was followed by his resurrection, "so we
walk in newness of life" (6:4). By sharing in the Christ event,
the believer has been "justified from sin" (6:7). Consequently,
the images of death and life dominate Paul's declaration as
Paul describes the irrevocability of the event that has created
a new corporate identity.[30]

The language is reminiscent of Paul's claim in other letters
that believers participate in the death of Christ and find a new
identity. In 2 Corinthians 5:14–15 Paul says, "One died for all,
therefore all died. And he died for all, so that those who live
may no longer live for themselves." And in Galatians 2:19 he
says, "I have been crucified with Christ." In Galatians 5:24,
those who belong to Christ "have crucified the flesh with its
desires." Believers have been transformed from the old existence
through their identification with the cross. Consequently, Paul
speaks of the finality of this change. Believers have put away the

29. See Gerd Theissen, "Die urchristliche Taufe und die soziale Konstrucktion
des neuen Menschen," in *Transformations of the Inner Self in Ancient Religions*, ed.
Jan Assmann and Guy G. Stroumsa, Studies in the History of Religions 83 (Leiden:
Brill, 1999), 105.
30. Ibid., 110.

body of sin at baptism (Rom. 6:6), dividing their lives between "then" and "now." Thus those who will ultimately bear the image of the glorified Christ (8:29) first experience the "likeness of his death" (6:5). By participating in the death, burial, and resurrection of Christ, they have overcome the power of sin that Paul described in 1:18–3:20.

Paul's declaration in 6:1–11 is likely to be problematic for a pastoral theology inasmuch as it raises this question: does Paul believe that Christians have completely overcome the power of sin? Paul's argument indicates that the continuing power of the old aeon still threatens believers. Despite this extraordinary claim that believers have put the body of sin to death (6:6), he adds, "So you also must *consider yourselves* dead to sin and alive to God in Christ Jesus" (6:11 NRSV). That is, the change of identity requires human cognition. Baptism does not produce an automatic transformation.[31] We find throughout the argument a pervasive appeal to the listeners' own knowledge of the events that have occurred.[32] Furthermore, the imperatives in 6:12–13 indicate that the desires of the body continue to be a reality as Christians still await the redemption of the body (8:23). Consequently, Paul instructs his listeners to actualize the new reality. We notice the emphasis on the body and its members, echoing Romans 1. Although they have entered the new creation, the power of the old creation is still present. Justification by faith includes not only the initial acceptance but the community's sustained obedience to God. Righteousness is not only one event but the power to which one makes the body available.

In 6:15–23 Paul repeats the call to actualize what one has already experienced. Again Paul appeals to the community's own story, recalling the defining event that has shaped it (6:17–18,

---

31. Engberg-Pedersen, *Paul and the Stoics*, 230–31.

32. See David Aune, "Human Nature and Ethics: Issues and Problems," in *Paul in His Hellenistic Context*, ed. Troels Engberg-Pedersen (Minneapolis: Fortress, 1995), 310. Cf. Rom. 6:6, "Knowing [*ginōskontes*] that our old self was crucified"; 6:8–9, "knowing that Christ, being raised from the dead, will never die." In Rom. 8, Paul speaks of those who "set their minds" on the things of the flesh or Spirit (8:5–6).

20–21). This event becomes the basis for the imperative in 6:19: "present your members as slaves to righteousness for sanctification" (NRSV), which is parallel to the imperative in 6:12–13 not to "present your members to sin as instruments of wickedness, but present yourselves to God as those who have been brought from death to life" (NRSV). Paul suggests here that the body is the expression of the self. Believers have overcome the passions of the body that Paul describes in 1:18–3:20. But their story is not complete, as the imperative indicates. Christians must actualize the event that has changed them.

Traditional outlines of Romans have often described Romans 1–5 under the heading of justification and Romans 6–8 under the heading of sanctification. This distinction is scarcely adequate in chapters 6–8, for sanctification (*hagiasmos*) is mentioned only twice (6:19, 22). Furthermore, justification and sanctification are closely intertwined in Paul's description of the Christian life, as we can see in his instruction to present our members "as slaves to righteousness for sanctification" (6:19). Elsewhere Paul speaks of both righteousness and sanctification as events in the community's past (cf. 1 Cor. 6:11). Here, however, righteousness is the power of the new aeon (cf. Rom. 6:13, 18, 20), and sanctification is the goal of this new existence. Paul takes this term from Israel's cultic life and applies it to Gentile Christians to describe the ethical life of believers as they turn away from the existence described in 1:18–3:20. Indeed, Paul employs *hagiasmos* in contrast to the "impurity" (*akatharsia*) (6:19) associated with sexual sins (cf. 1:24; 1 Thess. 4:7). He indicates the ethical implications of *hagiasmos* in Romans 6:22 when he speaks of the "fruit [*karpos*; NRSV, 'advantage'] of sanctification," which he contrasts to the previous existence in which the "fruit" (6:21; NRSV, "advantage") was death (cf. 7:5, "bear fruit to death"). Here *karpos* connotes the ethical results of one's existence (cf. Gal. 5:22; Rom. 1:13; Phil. 1:11, 22). The ultimate result of sanctification is "eternal life" (Rom. 6:22). Thus sanctification is the ongoing ethical transformation of the believer in anticipation of the end. As in 1 Thessalonians (3:13; 5:23), sanctification is

complete at the eschaton. The ultimate goal of Paul's ministry
therefore is to offer to God the Gentile community "sanctified
in the Holy Spirit" (Rom. 15:16).

The remainder of this unit indicates what sanctification
means for bodily existence. Although the indicatives in 6:1–11
indicate that sin has lost its power (6:14), the imperatives in
6:12–23 indicate that the body is still the seat of the passions
described in 1:18–32. In the listeners' own narrative, they have
been guilty of the vices mentioned in 1:18–32 (cf. 6:17–19)
but have already presented themselves to righteousness. The
paraenesis indicates that enslavement to the bodily passions
remains a possibility even if they have put to death the deeds
of the body. Believers overcome sin only when they actualize
what they already are. Paul demands an existence that is the
opposite of that described in 1:18–32.

Just as the entire narrative is divided between the "then"
and the "now" of God's actions (cf. 3:21), the community's
existence is similarly defined by the singular moment of baptism.
The listeners were "once" slaves of sin (6:17) and of impurity
(6:19) but have become slaves of righteousness (6:18). Those
who know the law have died to the law in order to belong to
another (7:4). All of the listeners struggled with the power
that the passions exercise over bodily existence, but they have
now entered a "newness of life" (6:4; 7:5–6) that marks the
end of the enslavement to the passions described in 1:18–3:20.
The community's story is not complete, however, for the end
of the narrative, as Paul indicates in 6:20, is eternal life, the
occasion when the community is ultimately transformed into
the image of the son.

Paul's pastoral challenge is to guide the community toward
this transformation. His concern is not about getting into a
relationship with God but about overcoming the power of sin
in order for transformation to take place. In Paul's emphasis
on the body and its members, he undoubtedly speaks of individuals. But he also attempts to form a new communal identity
for Gentile Christians who now share in a narrative that is not

yet complete. Baptism initiates the Christians into a "state of becoming" that is not complete until the end.[33]

7:7–25. Paul has indicated in Romans 6 that the believers overcome the power of the passions, and he demands that they now do the good as the means to transformation. He has not yet shown, however, how one who lives before the end actually overcomes the body's passions. In 7:7–8:13 he addresses this theme, expanding on the problem of willing and doing from Galatians 5:17 and continuing the discussion that he introduced in Romans 1:18–3:20, where he described the human dilemma that people do not act on their knowledge of the good. Earlier he has suggested that the law, instead of being the means of overcoming sin, in fact increases human sinfulness (cf. 4:15; 5:13; 7:5). This apparent equation of the law and sin raises the question of 7:7, "What shall we say? That the law is sin?" Paul not only answers this question in 7:7–25 but also advances the discussion of the human capacity to do the good.

In his use of the first-person singular, Paul is not speaking autobiographically but is describing a human dilemma, as we can see from the argument.[34] In 7:7–12 he speaks in the past tense of the emergence of sin, saying, "I would not have known desire [*epithymia*; NRSV, 'what it is to covet'] if the law had not said, 'You shall not desire' [NRSV, 'covet']." In quoting the Septuagint's tenth commandment (Exod. 20:17) against covetousness, he continues the focus on *epithymia* as the human problem. This comment is reminiscent of Romans 7:5,

---

33. Stuhlmacher, *Revisiting Paul's Doctrine*, 63.

34. Interpreters have identified several analogies to Paul's use of the first-person singular. U. Wilckens, *Der Brief an die Römer*, Evangelisch-katholischer Kommentar zum Neuen Testament, 3 vols. (Zurich: Neukirchener, 1978–1982), 2:277, points to parallels in the lament psalms and the *Hodayot* of the Dead Sea Scrolls. Stanley Stowers, *A Rereading of Romans* (New Haven: Yale University Press, 1994), identifies the literary style as "speech-in-character," where the speaker places a speech in the mouth of another character. See also Frank Thielman, "The Story of Israel and the Theology of Romans 5–8," in *Pauline Theology*, ed. Jouette M. Bassler, David M. Hay, and E. Elizabeth Johnson, 4 vols. (Minneapolis: Fortress, 1991–1997), 3:193. Thielman locates the first-person singular in the prayers of confession in Ezra 9:5–15; Neh. 9:6–37; Dan. 9:4–19. These passages, like Rom. 7:7–25, express anguish over the tendency to disobey God's law.

in which he has said of his listeners, "While we were living in the flesh, our sinful passions [*ta pathēmata tōn hamartiōn*], aroused by the law, were at work in our members" (NRSV). The "I" of the discussion therefore is the person under law. Paul echoes the Genesis story of the origin of sin (Gen. 3:13) when he says that "sin deceived me and through it [the commandment] killed me" (Rom. 7:11). Sin found its basis of operations and through the law brought death. Thus the law is not the answer to the problem of *epithymia*.

In 7:14–25 Paul moves to the present tense, elaborating on the problem of doing the good. Unlike believers in Romans 6 who have died to sin, Paul says, "I am of the flesh, sold into slavery under sin" (7:14 NRSV). Echoing familiar Greek maxims, he says, "For I do not do what I want, but I do the very thing I hate" (7:15), and repeats the same statement in 7:18–19, "I can will what is right and cannot do it. For I do not do the good that I want, but the evil that I hate is what I do."[35] The human dilemma is that of one who lives in the flesh (7:14, 18). He speaks of the problem of flesh (*sarx*, 7:14, 18) and of his members (7:23), and of the good intentions of his mind (*nous*, 7:23) and inmost self (*esō anthrōpos*, 7:22). This description is remarkably like that of 1:18–32, where "God gave them up" (1:24) to dishonor their bodies and to a "reprobate mind" (*nous*, 1:28). Thus the human dilemma, whether

35. Greek philosophical literature struggled with the problem of willing and doing. According to Socrates, "No one willingly does wrong" (Plato, *Protagoras* 345d–e; *Timaeus* 86d; *Laws* 731c, 860d). According to a widespread tradition, when humans are overcome by irrational impulses, they do wrong even when they know the right. Note Medea's speech in Euripides, *Medea* 1077–1080, when she killed her children: "But I am overcome by evil. Now I learn what evil deeds I intended to perform; but passion [*thymos*] overpowered my wishes, which is the cause of the greatest evil for mortals." See David Aune, "Two Pauline Models of the Person," in *The Whole and Divided Self*, ed. David Aune and John McCarthy (New York: Crossroad, 1997), 97. See also Stowers, *Rereading of Romans*, 260–72, for Greek reflection on the divided self and the overcoming of the passions. See also Petra von Gemünden, "Die urchristliche Taufe und der Umgang mit den Affekten," in *Transformations of the Inner Self in Ancient Religions*, ed. Jan Assmann and Guy G. Stroumsa, Studies in the History of Religions 83 (Leiden: Brill, 1999), 124–29, for the response of Hellenistic Jewish writers to the problem of the passions.

one keeps the law or does not, is the incapacity of mind and body to do the good.

8:1–13. Although Paul has instructed the Gentile Christians to overcome the passions of the body, he has still not indicated how this is possible insofar as the law is not the means for human transformation. In 8:1–13 Paul gives the answer. Those who have been enslaved by sin have now been liberated by the law of the Spirit (8:1–2). In 8:3–4 Paul explains the new situation. God has overcome the weakness of the flesh by sending his son in the flesh "so that the just requirement of the law might be fulfilled in us, who walk not according to the flesh but according to the Spirit" (NRSV).

Once more Paul appeals to the concept of interchange (cf. p. 25) to declare that the coming of Christ created the possibility of a new humanity in which we might become like Christ. Those who share in the death of Christ (6:1–11) are now able to meet God's demands. The Christian community keeps the just requirement of the law, thus fulfilling the requirement that the doers of the law be justified (2:13). The new dimension to existence is the presence of the Spirit, the power of the new age. Paul introduced the Spirit as the eschatological gift in 5:5 and in 7:6, where he indicated that in the new existence we are slaves "in the newness of the Spirit and not in the oldness of the letter." Paul's claim probably rests on his reading of Jeremiah 31:33, according to which the new age will be the occasion when God will "put [God's] law within them, and [God] will write it on their hearts." The community therefore fulfills the law of God. Unlike the wretched man of Romans 7, who is incapacitated by the sin that lives within him, the new being in Romans 8 is empowered by the Christ who lives within (8:9). This Spirit empowers the community and "gives life to [their] mortal bodies" (8:11). The community is able to overcome the passions of the body because of the power of the Spirit.

In Romans, as in Paul's earlier letters, human transformation requires the empowerment of the Spirit. Here one sees an expansion of Galatians 5–6. As in Galatians, divine empowerment requires a human response. The old aeon remains a possibility. Hence Paul concludes this unit with the paraenesis of 8:12–13. The community that is empowered by the Spirit is now indebted to live according to the Spirit. The community faces the choice, and Paul attempts to guide them.

We may assume that those who are transformed into the image of Christ (8:29) are first transformed by the overcoming of the passions of bodily existence and the appropriation of the power of the new aeon. To believe is therefore not only to come into the faith but to be conformed to the image of the crucified Christ. To be baptized is to share the existence of the crucified one.

9:1–11:36

The remainder of Paul's argument in Romans is a challenge for the community to recognize the significance of the Christ event for continued Christian existence. In chapters 9–11 Paul indicates once more his deep pastoral engagement with his listeners as he reflects on the Israelites who have not believed his message (9:1–5). Because they have not met the requirement that "all who call on the Lord will be saved" (10:1–13, here 10:13), Paul must address the apparent failure of God's word (9:6, 10). Paul answers that the present situation does not reflect God's failure but that in the call of the Gentiles God has acted as he did in Israel's past, choosing to show mercy apart from deeds (9:6–29). Gentiles have, in fact, met the conditions of righteousness by faith (10:1–21). The current situation is not, however, irrevocable, for Israel's rejection is only temporary (11:1–12).

Paul's argument is not, as it has often been interpreted, a theoretical reflection on God's purposes but the basis for his appeal to Gentile readers, as 11:13–36 indicates. He reminds them that their election should not be a source of arrogance; they are merely limbs that have been grafted on to the olive tree by the grace of God. Consequently, Paul says, "Do not boast over the branches. If you do boast, remember that it is not you that support the root, but the root that supports you" (11:18

NRSV). This counsel against boasting recalls Paul's earlier statement that those who keep the law have no basis for boasting (3:27–4:2). Just as God grafted the Gentiles to the olive tree, he can again graft Israel back to the tree (11:23). Because of God's sovereign plan for the salvation of the world, Paul introduces his extraordinary claim that "all Israel will be saved" (11:26) with the words "So that you may not claim to be wiser than you are" (11:25 NRSV). Thus the difficult and tortuous argument of chapters 9–11 serves a paraenetic purpose: to demonstrate that the mercy of God undermines the arrogance that divides communities. In his ministry Paul hopes to present a people to God at the end time. His work will be complete only if it is a unified community of Jews and Gentiles.

12:1–15:13

Romans 9–11 points toward God's ultimate work of salvation for Jews and Gentiles. In 12:1–15:13 Paul describes the life of the community as it awaits God's ultimate victory. Here we see not the addendum to Romans but the climax of the argument for the believing community. Paul calls on the Romans to join him in implementing in their own house churches the pastoral vision that he has expressed in the preceding argument.[36] Paul's request, "Present your bodies a living sacrifice, holy and acceptable to God" (12:1), is the consequence of the argument. Here, as he continues the argument of 6:1–8:13, Paul shows how the conditions of humanity in 1:18–3:20 have been overcome. Whereas humanity under the wrath of God "dishonors the body" (1:24), the new humanity presents the body as a sacrifice to God. Unlike those who worshiped the creature rather than the creator, the new humanity offers spiritual worship. The community that will ultimately be transformed (*hous . . . proōrisen symmorphous*, 8:29), is instructed to "be transformed by the renewing of the mind" (12:2). Those who were initiated into the death and resurrection of Christ in the

---

36. Crafton, "Paul's Rhetorical Vision," 334.

singular event of baptism are engaged in a continuing process of change. The passive voice (*metamorphousthe*) indicates that the community cooperates in the work of God.[37] The *nous* is no longer perverted or in despair (cf. 7:25). The result is that they may "discern what is the will of God" (*eis to dokimazein . . . to thelēma tou theou*, 12:2), unlike the humanity described in 1:18–3:20.

In the paraeneses of 12:1–15:13 and 6:12–23, Paul offers a means of doing the will of God that does not involve the works of the law. In both instances this new existence includes the appropriate presentation of the body to God (cf. 6:12–13). Whereas Paul's primary concern is the overcoming of the passions through the power of the Spirit in chapters 6 and 7, in 12:1–15:13 Paul turns in a new direction to describe the transformed existence. Here he demonstrates how this transformed existence entails the overcoming of the antisocial vices listed in 1:29–31 through a new orientation of the self. The dominant motif of 12:1–15:13 is the surrender of individual identity for the sake of others. The opening exhortation "not to think more highly than you ought to think" (12:3) draws the consequences of Paul's gospel of God's righteousness for all, as Paul has indicated earlier with his claim that there is no basis for boasting (3:27–4:2). Thus Paul draws the consequences of the argument in Romans 9–11, describing the existence of a new people that has overcome ethnic privilege in order to live together as a community.[38] The reorientation of the self includes a redirection away from the body's passions and self-centeredness and toward a concern for others.

This directedness toward others is evident in the life within the community, where all privileges are surrendered for the sake of others. Within the context of Romans, Paul's instruction on the body of Christ (12:3–8) is a reminder that a divided humanity overcomes the antisocial vices of 1:29–32 within

37. J. M. Nützel, "*metamorphoō*," in *Exegetical Dictionary of the New Testament*, ed. H. Balz and G. Schneider, 3 vols. (Grand Rapids, 1990–1993), 2:415.

38. James D. G. Dunn, "Romans 13:1–7—a Charter for Political Quietism?" *Ex auditu* 2 (1986): 61.

the body of Christ. If the righteousness of God extends to all, Paul assumes that they will live neither in separate enclaves nor in individual isolation but as members of the corporate body. Since Paul's argument removes the law as a boundary separating the ethnic groups, he now proceeds to redefine the ethical characteristics of the new community.[39]

Paul's words "Let love be genuine" (12:9) and his instruction to "love one another" (13:8) frame the discussion in chapters 12–13. Indeed, Paul summarizes these chapters with the statements that "the one who loves another has fulfilled the law" (13:8) and "love is the fulfilling of the law" (13:10). In this sense Paul's listeners become the community of "doers of the law" who will receive the ultimate vindication (2:13). Through the power of the Spirit, they fulfill the just demand of the law (8:4). Thus, although Paul's community is not bound by the works of the law that separate Jew and Gentile, his community fulfills the demand of the law. Transformation involves living by the love command.

This love for others is evident in the specific instructions that Paul gives (12:9–18). Paul expands on the paraeneses of earlier letters to describe the deeds of the new community with the language drawn from family life. They are "devoted to one another in brotherly love [NRSV, 'with mutual affection']" (12:10; cf. 1 Thess. 4:9).[40] Paul uses the language of family life, as in the earlier letters, to describe the existence within the community of faith.[41] The result will be a pattern of life very similar to the one that Paul describes in Philippians. Members

---

39. Ibid., 63.

40. *Tē philadelphia eis allēlous philostorgoi* focuses on familial love. Cf. C. Spicq, *Theological Lexicon of the New Testament*, 3 vols. (Peabody, MA: Hendrickson, 1994), 3.462–64: "In common usage, *philostorgia* has the more positive sense of the mother's innate love, benevolence, and devotion toward her children; than that of a husband for his wife or a wife for her husband; of a father for his sons and of sons for a father. But *philostorgia* is also used for all links of kinship, even one's attachment to guest-friends (*SEG* XVIII, 143, 69), or the attachment of slaves to their masters."

41. See H. Moxnes, "The Quest for Honor and Unity of the Community in Romans 12," in *Paul in His Hellenistic Context*, ed. Troels Engberg-Pedersen (Minneapolis: Fortress, 1995), 225.

of the community will "outdo one another in showing honor" (Rom. 12:10; cf. Phil. 2:3, "in humility counting others better than yourselves") and "live in harmony with one another" (Rom. 12:16; cf. Phil. 2:2) as they "associate with the lowly" without being "wise among themselves" (Rom. 12:16). This directedness toward others extends outside the community and includes conduct that "is noble in the sight of all" (12:17). Paul echoes the Synoptic tradition (cf. Matt. 5:44), offering a specific illustration of existence under the love commandment with the advice on nonresistance toward evildoers. His comments on submission to the government (Rom. 13:1–7) also offer an illustration of the practical significance of the love command. Rather than assert themselves, believers will live within the structures of society, pay their taxes (13:7), and contribute to the good of others. As in other paraeneses, Paul extends to those who are outside the community of faith the Christian devotion to others (cf. Gal. 6:10; 1 Thess. 4:9–12).

The concluding instruction of this unit, "Put on the Lord Jesus Christ, and make no provision for the flesh, to gratify its desires" (Rom. 13:14 NRSV), frames the discussion that began in 12:1–2 and continues the concern with the passions of the flesh, a concern that is present throughout Romans. Paul employs baptismal language (cf. Gal. 3:27) to encourage believers to recognize the path to overcoming the passions. Those who are baptized find their new corporate identity that enables them to overcome the self-centeredness described in Romans 1:18–3:20.

In 14:1–15:13 Paul reaches the conclusion to the long argument and gives a specific instance of the implications of his doctrine of righteousness for community formation. The discussion is framed by the imperatives "Welcome those who are weak in faith" (ton asthenounta tē pistei, 14:1) and "welcome one another" (proslambanesthe allēlous, 15:7), followed by the reasons for this conduct. The ensuing argument indicates that major ethnic and cultural differences inhibit the formation of the familial atmosphere described in 12:1–13:14. Paul's movement from the distinction between strong and weak (14:1;

15:7) to that between Jew and Gentile (15:1–13) suggests that Paul envisions here, as in his other churches, the problem of community formation. In the imperatives of 14:1; 15:1, he challenges Jews and Gentiles to welcome one another into their own house churches.[42] Here Paul adapts what he has said to the Corinthians (1 Cor. 8:1–13; 10:14–11:1) to the problem of creating a community composed of Jews and Gentiles. In Romans 14:1–15:13 Paul supports his instructions, speaking to the strong (14:1; 15:1) and to everyone within the community (14:13), demonstrating why they should defer to each other.

In 14:1–12 Paul elaborates on the argument of the letter, arguing, as in 2:1–16, that everyone stands under the judgment of God. Paul builds on the entire letter to urge that members of the community neither judge nor despise each other, and he appeals to what he has established already: that the death of Christ establishes the identity of Christians, who no longer live for themselves (14:7). As a result of baptism, which initiates believers into a shared story, all recognize a new identity marked by self-denial and a new existence in Christ. Moreover, as in chapter 2, "each of us will give an account of ourselves to God" (14:12).

This concern for others becomes especially the obligation of the strong, whom Paul directs not to put a stumbling block or hindrance in the way of the other, for one must walk according to love, which entails not destroying one for whom Christ died (14:15). Consequently, they are to pursue peace and mutual upbuilding (14:19). Thus the decisions are determined by a concrete example of living according to the love command (cf. 13:8–10).

Paul summarizes the argument of this unit in 15:1–13 in two parallel exhortations (15:1–6, 7–13), which also function as summaries of the entire letter. In each instance Paul calls for acceptance of the other and then appeals to the Christ event and to Scripture as a warrant for the conduct. This is followed in each instance by a prayer for what he expects of the commu-

42. See Bauer, Danker, Arndt, and Gingrich, *Greek-English Lexicon*, 883.

nity. In this dual conclusion, one sees the force of the argument recapitulated for the sake of communal concerns.

In 15:1–6 Paul identifies himself with the strong, indicating that the obligation is "not to please ourselves" (15:1). He adds, "Each should please his neighbor and do what is good for upbuilding" (cf. 14:19). The Christians are directed to others within the community. This instruction is a paraphrase of the love command. The warrant is that "Christ did not please himself" (15:3), an idea that Paul supports with the appeal to Scripture. Thus the Christ event defines Christian behavior. One may recall 14:8–10 and its echo of chapter 6. The Christian community is defined by the death of Jesus. Paul's argument is similar to his exhortation in Philippians 2:1–11, where he speaks in the imperative, "Do nothing out of selfish ambition and conceit" (Phil. 2:3), and then offers the self-emptying of Christ as the warrant for Christian behavior. To die with Christ is to deny oneself for the sake of others. The end result, as the prayer in Romans 15:5–6 indicates, is that a community from disparate backgrounds is "to live in harmony" (*to auto phronein*) despite their fundamental differences. Paul's goal—indeed the goal of his ministry— is that together they "glorify God with one voice." His pastoral goal is a community bound together in love.

In 15:7–13 Paul reaches the conclusion of the argument, repeating the substance of 15:1–6 and summarizing the content of the letter. The command "Receive one another as Christ received you" repeats the focus on receiving each other and again appeals to the Christ event. Christ received both groups in his atoning sacrifice and death. Again Paul elaborates on the Christ event by saying that Christ became a *diakonos* (15:8). Christ is a servant of both Jews and Gentiles. That is, Christ is the one who brings them together.

Here we see the relationship between Paul's pastoral ambition in 15:15–16 and the argument of the letter. Paul's pastoral ambition is the offering of the nations to God. This offering includes a community in which Gentiles are not alone but take their place alongside the Jews. His argument serves the purpose of strengthening the community and reminding it of the gospel for all. Only a community "transformed" morally will be transformed into the image of Christ at the eschaton.

Conclusion: The Pastoral Significance of Romans

Paul's pastoral theology in Romans is evident in the intersection between his articulation of his mission (1:5; 15:15–20) and the argument of the letter, which is intended to support this pastoral ambition. His goal is the eschatological offering of the Gentiles, sanctified in the Spirit (15:16). This offering presupposes not only the evangelization of the community but its transformation. In Paul's pastoral theology, the community of faith participates in Israel's grand narrative, which includes creation (cf. 5:12–21) and a new creation (cf. 8:18–39) when God's people will be transformed into the image of the Son. In the meantime, God has already vindicated the believing community (5:1; 8:1) in anticipation of the ultimate salvation when Paul will present the Gentiles as an offering to God. By participating in the Christ event (6:1–11), the church experiences the new aeon when God triumphs over sin but waits for the ultimate redemption.

This unfinished narrative is the framework for Paul's pastoral theology. We live with grief and threatening forces as we wait for God's righteousness (8:18–39). Although we have irrevocably been delivered from the body's impulses (6:6), the old existence remains a threatening possibility. The ultimate transformation has not taken place, and Paul's goal remains incomplete. Paul's challenge is to ensure the transformation of the community as the prelude for his offering the "sacrifice of the Gentiles" (15:16), and his work will be complete only when the listeners respond to his pastoral vision.

Paul's theology of transformation in 5–8 and 12:1–15:13 provides valuable insights for a contemporary pastoral theology. In the first place, although he articulates a theology of God's acceptance of sinners (Rom. 1–4), as pastoral theologians have long maintained, his doctrine of grace is not the center of his theology in the letter but the foundation for the later argument. In the climax of the letter in 12:1–15:13, Paul calls on the community to live out the implications of the gospel and to be transformed by renewal of the mind, thus overcoming the corruption of mind and body described in Romans 1. A theology of transformation continues to be an important foundation for pastoral theology. Although a theology of grace remains an important dimension of pastoral theology, this perspective is not helpful without a theology of transformation that challenges believers to overcome human failures through the resources of the Christian faith.

In the second place, as we have learned from Paul, transformation occurs where the community is constantly reminded of the story that called it into existence. When the story of the cross becomes our story, reminding us of the one who did not please himself, we find a new identity, abandoning the self-centeredness of our own culture and adopting an orientation toward others as the basis for our own communities. Our transformation remains incomplete as long as we live in isolation or in homogeneous enclaves. It remains incomplete in our own congregations as we battle over worship styles or divide into competitive interest groups intent on winning. Paul's aim that the community composed of different cultural backgrounds "glorify God with one voice" remains a pastoral goal today. This transformation can occur only when we reaffirm the story of the cross as the story of our congregation.

In the third place, Christian formation involves Christian identity and ethics. As argued here about Romans 7, Paul does not build a pastoral theology on the basis of our acceptance that we each remain "simul justus et peccator"—both justified and sinner at the same time. Paul argues that transformation is already occurring and that the community now "fulfills the just requirement of the law" (8:4) through the power of the Spirit, overcoming the culture's self-absorption. Paul does not say, however, that Christians are incapable of returning to the former enslavement to temptation or that they do not sin. He argues that they may now live under the reign of righteousness as they "walk by the Spirit" (8:5–8). The Christian faith offers the resources for doing the will of God (cf. 12:2).

Although Paul does not offer comprehensive ethical instruction, he provides examples of the conduct that is appropriate to those who have died with Christ. Paul envisions a counter-cultural community that, empowered by the Spirit to do the will of God, lives out the consequences of the gospel. A Pauline pastoral theology will include the ethical transformation of a community, providing guidelines for behavior that are founded on the Christ event.

In the fourth place, Paul's pastoral theology is ecclesiocentric and eschatological. Ministry is not done in isolation, and the goal of the pastor is not only the well-being of the individual. The goal of ministry is to ensure that individuals discover the resources for transformation within the community and that corporate well-being is the goal of the pastor. The eschatological dimension is important insofar as we direct our corporate priorities toward the ultimate goals, recognizing that eschatology places all of the issues of congregational life in perspective. The church has seen a glimpse of the end of the narrative, when it will be transformed into the image of the Son. To be engaged in ministry is to work with God toward this goal.

Although there are shortcomings in the traditional appeal to Romans for a pastoral theology, the letter provides a profound basis for our own understanding of the ministerial task. Because of the distance that separates us from Paul and his churches, we cannot simply transfer his words to our own time without considerable hermeneutical reflection. Nevertheless, Paul provides a framework for our own reflection on the nature and goals of ministry. Our task is to work with God to ensure that we complete the final chapter of the narrative of God. The narrative is complete when the community has been transformed by the cross.

5

Building the Community

Pastoral Theology as Community Formation in the Corinthian Letters

The letters of Paul address communities in the middle of a corporate narrative that has both a beginning and an end, and they provide a snapshot of a particular moment in Paul's pastoral work with his churches. The Corinthian letters, however, provide a filmstrip rather than a snapshot inasmuch as they record distinct stages in Paul's stormy relationship with this church. Although scholars dispute the number of letters now contained in 1 and 2 Corinthians (i.e., whether 2 Corinthians is a composite of two or more letters), what is not in dispute is that the letters reflect several stages in Paul's interaction with the Corinthians over a period of approximately six years. During this period Paul wrote a series of letters in response to issues that emerged after he left Corinth. His eighteen months of pastoral leadership (cf. Acts 18:12) among the new converts were insufficient for the shaping of the Corinthian church, for new questions arose after he left. At the last stage of Paul's series of visits and letters, the success of his ministry is still in doubt. He fears that the same quarreling, jealousy, anger, and sexual immorality that characterized the Corinthians in their spiritual infancy will continue to be present (cf. 1 Cor. 3:1–5; 2 Cor. 12:20–21). Nevertheless, he continues his argument in the hope of persuading the Corinthians to become the community that he envisions. At the end of 2 Corinthians, Paul's pastoral work remains unfinished business.

The nature of pastoral leadership is a major topic of conversation in 1 Corinthians (cf. 1 Cor. 1–4) and the fundamental issue in 2 Corinthians. In contrast to the other letters, however, the focus in the Corinthian letters—especially 2 Corinthians—is on Paul's ministerial credentials. He does not articulate his pastoral vision through paraenetic instructions in the same way that he does in the other letters, shaping his argument to focus on the future conduct of his communities. Nevertheless, although the focus of the argument in the Corinthian letters is on Paul and the specific questions raised by that community, these letters provide not only a defense of Paul's ministry but a vision of the end result that will determine the success of his ministry.

The Pastoral Situation in the Corinthian Letters

One may assume that Paul's stay in Corinth provided ample time for him to strengthen the foundation of the church. Indeed, 1 Corinthians gives significant evidence of extensive catechetical work by Paul during that time.[1] Despite the instruction that Paul gave the Corinthians, he received information soon after he left Corinth that his work was in jeopardy (cf. 1 Cor. 1:11; 5:1; 7:1). His remarkable attempt to build a cohesive community out of people from different ethnic groups and social levels was now threatened by divisiveness and partisanship (1:10–17; 3:1–5). Although Paul responds to several discrete

1. Note the appeals to the traditions already delivered to the Corinthians (11:23–26; 15:3–4). Note also Paul's frequent appeals to what the community already knows (cf. 6:2, 3, 9, 15–16).

problems in the Corinthian church, the many issues appear to be symptoms of one underlying problem: many of the members of the Corinthian church conduct themselves on the basis of the cultural values of Roman Corinth.[2] Although they do not deny the basic Christian confessions (cf. 8:6; 15:1–3, 12), they now interpret the Christian message on the basis of inherited cultural mores.[3]

Behind the issues of sexuality and marriage (5:1–13; 6:12–7:40), Christian interaction with idolatry (8:1–11:1), and corporate worship (11:2–14:40) is the underlying problem of the arrogance of Corinthians who celebrate wisdom, rhetoric, and individual freedom in a way that undermines the unity of the community.[4] With their slogan, "All things are lawful" (*panta exestin*, 6:12; 10:23), they declare their independence from others, challenge Paul's leadership (4:1–13), and claim the right to do as they please.[5] The issues originate primarily from the socially pretentious members of the congregation, who manifest a partisan affiliation with their teachers, create jealousy and strife among some members (1:11; 3:1–5), and take less fortunate members before pagan courts (6:1–11). As people of privilege, they claim the right (*exousia*, 8:9) to attend banquets with pagans (8:1–11:1), where sexual promiscuity was commonplace.[6] At the Lord's Supper, this influential minority shames those who have nothing (11:22). These issues reflect

2. Bruce Winter, *After Paul Left Corinth* (Grand Rapids: Eerdmans, 2001), 27.

3. J. Becker, *Paul: Apostle to the Gentiles* (Louisville: Westminster/John Knox, 1993), 199: "This Corinthian development took place under the conditions of a newly arisen Gentile-Christian church, which did not simply lay aside its former culture, understanding of religion, and interpretation of the world, nor did it adapt itself fully to the apostle's understanding during Paul's stay in Corinth."

4. Stephen M. Pogoloff, *Logos and Sophia: The Rhetorical Situation of 1 Corinthians*, Society of Biblical Literature Dissertation Series 134 (Atlanta: Scholars Press, 1992), 113–19.

5. See Peter Marshall, *Enmity at Corinth*, Wissenschaftliche Untersuchungen zum Neuen Testament 2.23 (Tübingen: J. C. B. Mohr, 1987), 189.

6. Winter, *After Paul Left Corinth*, 88, rightly points out that Paul does not mention brothels. The involvement with prostitutes mentioned in 6:12–20 is more likely associated with the banquets described in 8:1–13.

less a coherent theological position than the arrogance and anticommunal outlook of many of the Corinthians.[7]

In 2 Corinthians, the situation has been exacerbated by the arrival of opposing ministers who display the qualities of leadership admired in Corinth and join forces with those who already challenge the legitimacy of Paul's ministry (cf. 1 Cor. 4:5). Some of the issues that Paul faced in 1 Corinthians, including his oratorical ability (cf. 1 Cor. 1:17–2:5) and refusal to accept patronage (cf. 1 Cor. 4:11–12) continue in 2 Corinthians (cf. 2 Cor. 10:1, 10–11; 11:7–11). In addition, new issues emerge in the opponents' insistence on professional boasting and their rival claims to be "ministers of Christ" (2 Cor. 11:23).[8] Because Paul has been forced into self-praise by the opponents' own boasts and the Corinthians' openness to their claims, the primary issue of 2 Corinthians is Paul's own qualification as a minister of Christ. Paul's pastoral theology becomes evident when he describes his pastoral ambitions for this church as he defends his ministry.

Although Paul, as the founder of the Corinthian church, might have expected to define the nature of pastoral ministry without offering an explanation, the partisanship among the Corinthians and the presence of rival teachers forced him into a sustained description of his pastoral ambitions in both letters. In the Corinthian letters, the community's openness to secular definitions of leadership require Paul to articulate his pastoral theology. His personal defense is the occasion for describing the goals for his pastoral work.

Paul's Pastoral Theology in 1 Corinthians

Paul's salutation (1:1–3) and thanksgiving (1:4–9) anticipate the major themes of the letter and establish his pastoral vision for the church. In addressing the *ekklēsia* at Corinth, he indicates

7. Pogoloff, *Logos and Sophia*, 104.
8. E. A. Judge, "Paul's Boasting in Relation to Contemporary Professional Practice," *Australian Biblical Review* 10 (1968): 46–47.

the corporate nature of his pastoral work and communication. He presents a corporate narrative of a church that stands on the middle ground between its founding and its completion. The redundant address, "those who are being sanctified in Christ Jesus, called to be saints [*klētois hagiois*]" (1:2), indicates the significance of both the past and the present in the community's corporate narrative and anticipates an important dimension of the pastoral theology of the letter. As in 6:11, the passive voice, "sanctified" (*hēgiasmenois*), here indicates that God has set the community apart at the beginning of its corporate existence, making it a part of Israel's grand narrative as God's holy people (cf. Lev. 19:2). The use of the perfect tense indicates that God's sanctifying act in the past has continuing results.

In the opening thanksgiving (1 Cor. 1:4–9), Paul's pastoral theology is evident in his use of three verb tenses to describe the activity of God and the corporate narrative of the community. His repeated use of the second-person plural solidifies the corporate identity of a community torn by factions. In 1:4–6 Paul speaks in the aorist tense, expressing thanks for what God has done in the past, indicating that the existence of the community is the result not of human activity but of "the grace given to you." The evidence of God's grace is the fact that the entire community has "been enriched in every way" just as "the testimony of Christ has been confirmed among you" (1:6). The use of the aorist passives *eploutisthēte* ("you have become rich") and *ebebaiōthē* ("has been confirmed") also indicates that God is the source of the community's gifts in the past. With his emphasis on the corporate dimension of God's grace, he challenges Corinthian factionalism, indicating that their riches "in speech and knowledge of every kind" (1:5) are not the possession of isolated individuals but the property of the entire community as it receives God's grace. In a manner characteristic of the *exordium* of a speech, he addresses the issues at Corinth indirectly and in a manner calculated to make the listeners favorably disposed.

The present tense, "you do not lack any spiritual gift" (1:7), also alludes to a controversy at Corinth and anticipates Paul's later argument (1 Cor. 12–14), as he refers to the continuation of the church's corporate narrative into the present time, emphasizing that the gifts belong to the entire community. Paul also speaks in the present to describe the community's anticipation of the end of the narrative ("as you await the revelation of Christ"), and he speaks in the future tense to describe God's role in bringing the narrative toward its goal. The same God who brought the community into being by his grace will sustain it to the end, for God "will strengthen you to the end, so that you will be blameless at the day of our Lord Jesus Christ." Just as the testimony of Christ has been strengthened (*ebebaiōthē*) by God, he will "strengthen" (*bebaiōsei*, 1:8) the Corinthians. Thus the church now shares in Israel's narrative, with its hope for the final day when the story will come to the end. God's faithfulness in initiating the church's corporate narrative (1:9) is the basis for Paul's confident expectation for the church's future (cf. Phil. 1:6). Paul's use of three verb tenses in 1:4–9 reflects his understanding of the corporate narrative, for the church now stands between God's acts in the past and those in the future. His thanksgiving for what God has done in the past (1:4–6) is the basis (*hōste*) for the community's present (1:7) and confident expectation of God's acts in the future.

Although Paul does not mention his own role in the pastoral ministry, he sets the stage for the later discussion by indicating that he and the community stand within an incomplete corporate narrative in which God is the primary actor. Paul's pastoral vision is evident in his hope that the community will ultimately be "blameless" (*anegklētos*, 1:8) at the end. Although the term *anegklētos* appears elsewhere only in Colossians 1:22 to describe the vision for the ultimate destination of the church, similar language appears in Paul's other prayers. In Philippians 1:10 he prays that the community become "pure and blameless" (*eilikrineis kai aproskopoi*) on the day of Christ, and in 1 Thessalonians 3:13 he prays that they will be "blameless" (*amemptoi*) at the coming of Christ. Although three different Greek words are rendered "blameless" by the NRSV, each word denotes ethical transformation. In its present condition, the community has not reached the goal, for it must progress from its infancy (cf. 1 Cor. 3:1–5) to maturity. The community's conversion is therefore only the beginning of the narrative. Paul does not envision blameless individuals but a community transformed by God.

The remainder of 1 Corinthians demonstrates that the conditions at Corinth now frustrate Paul's pastoral vision. Despite the suggestion that the community's present experience in the corporate narrative is one of being sanctified (1:2) and enriched (1:5, 7), the remainder of the letter indicates that the present tense of the community is marked by obstacles to its progress. Paul writes to ensure that his pastoral vision of a church blameless at the parousia will become a reality. In 1:10 he states the thesis (*propositio*) to be argued, and in 1:11–17 he gives a brief summary of recent events (*narratio*), setting the stage for the argument (*probatio*) that follows in 1:18–15:58.

The Fundamentals of Paul's Pastoral Theology (1:18–4:21)

After shaming the Corinthians for their factions (1:11–17), he challenges their secular point of view by offering a new epistemology in 1:18–2:16, explaining that the cross reveals a wisdom unintelligible to those who do not posses the Spirit and is a challenge to the wisdom that they celebrate.[9] He then claims that the Corinthian factions are evidence that they have not advanced toward the goal of transformation. As "fleshly" (*sarkikoi*) people (3:3), they are no different from the "natural" (*psychikos*, 2:14) people who do not understand divine wisdom. As "children" (*nēpioi*, 3:1) who divide into factions, they have not advanced beyond the time of their conversion. Their attachment to leaders is a sign of partisanship and a demonstration that they have not grown.

9. Charles Cousar, "The Theological Task of 1 Corinthians," in *Pauline Theology*, ed. Jouette M. Bassler, David M. Hay, and E. Elizabeth Johnson, 4 vols. (Minneapolis: Fortress, 1991–1997), 2:94–96. See also Victor Paul Furnish, "Theology in 1 Corinthians," ibid., 2:67–68.

In 3:5–4:5 Paul offers a vision of the role of ministers that is an alternative to the secular model advocated by the Corinthians. His model demonstrates the role of the minister in the transformation of the community. In 3:5 Paul indicates that he and Apollos do not regard each other as rivals[10] but as servants (*diakonoi*) through whom the Corinthians have believed in the same master (*kyrios*). One may compare Paul's additional description of their role in 4:1, where they are "servants of Christ and stewards of God's mysteries" (*hypēretas Christou kai oikonomous mystēriōn theou*), commissioned by God. Thus Paul challenges the Corinthians' focus on leaders by using the self-effacing language of slavery. Although he and Apollos have different functions—Paul planted and Apollos watered—they are united as slaves of God. Over against the partisan rivalry of the Corinthians, the major actor is God, who has given them their ministries (3:5). The repetition of the words "God gave the increase" in 3:7–8 indicates that the emphasis is on God's work of shaping the community. This emphasis on God is continued in 3:9, where Paul includes the Corinthians in his metaphor. In the phrase "You are God's field, God's building" (*theou geōrgion, theou oikodomē este*), the emphasis rests, as the Greek word order indicates, on the fact that the community is *God's* building. Apostles are nothing but assistants and helpers of God.[11] With the dual metaphor of the vineyard and the building, Paul alludes to Jeremiah's description of God's role of building and planting the exiles of Judah (Jer. 24:6).[12] This emphasis on the role of God is a challenge to the Corinthians' emphasis on leaders. Furthermore, Paul's corporate understanding is evident in his insistence that God's building is not the individual but the community.

10. David Kuck, "Paul and Pastoral Ambition: A Reflection on 1 Corinthians 3–4," *Currents in Theology and Mission* 19 (1992): 176.

11. W. Schrage, *Der erste Brief an die Korinther*, 4 vols., Evangelisch-katholischer Kommentar zum Neuen Testament 7 (Neukirchen-Vluyn: Neukirchener Verlag, 1991–2001), 1:294.

12. Cf. also Jer. 31:4, 28; 33:7.

With the transition of the metaphor from the vineyard to the building in 1 Corinthians 3:9, Paul now develops his pastoral theology in explicit terms, in 3:10–17 applying to the church a familiar image of the people of God as a building.[13] This image becomes the leitmotif of the entire letter, as we shall see. Paul's task in the extended metaphor of the building in 3:10–17 is to challenge Corinthian partisanship by describing his relationship to other ministers who are engaged in the building process. The entire argument is an elaboration of Paul's affirmation in 3:10. He refers to his own distinctive role in the building project, describing himself (3:10) as the "wise architect" who laid the foundation in the past while other ministers continue to "build on" (*epoikodomei*).[14] Here, as in Romans 15:20, Paul's task is to lay the foundation, not to build on the work of another. In 2 Corinthians he describes his role as that of "building up" the people of God (2 Cor. 10:8). To lay the foundation is to establish the corporate community. This description of a church under construction continues Paul's earlier indication that the church lives in the present, with its corporate narrative between the past and the future. Until the building project is completed, builders will continue to build on. Paul's role as "wise architect" is analogous to his role as planter (1 Cor. 3:6) or father (4:14–21) to the church. The others who build on include Apollos and other ministers. Paul's claim that "there is no other foundation that can be laid" (3:11) interrupts the flow of the argument but reminds the partisans of their excessive interest in the ministers.

Despite Paul's confidence in 1:8 that "God will confirm you to the end blameless at the day of Christ," his warning in 3:10–17 points out the obstacles to the church's successful completion of the narrative. The laying of the foundation does not ensure that the community will be blameless at the end, for the community depends on the quality of the work done by those who build on, and Paul fears that the other contractors

13. Cf. Ps. 28:5; 122:3; 147:2; Jer. 31:4, 28, 38; 33:7.
14. On the distinctive task of the architect, see J. Duncan Derrett, "Paul as Master-Builder," *Evangelical Quarterly* 69 (1997): 130–31.

are "botching the subsequent construction job."[15] Thus the central focus of Paul's building imagery in 3:10–17 is 3:10c, "Each builder must choose with care how to build on it," for the remainder of this unit is an elaboration of this warning. Some builders use inferior materials, and the quality of the workmanship will "become visible" on the "day" when the work will be tested (3:13). Paul contrasts the work that abides (*menei*) with that which will be "burned up" (*katakaēsetai*, 3:14–15). Work done with inferior materials will not survive. Paul refers to the "day" (cf. 1:8; 5:5) that will test the quality of the ministers' work. Although we do not know how far to push Paul's imagery, the primary focus is evident: only the "day" will reveal the quality of the work.

According to 3:10–17, the laying of the foundation is only the beginning of a long process, for the building remains under construction until the day of Christ. The focus of the passage is on Paul's successors—other ministers—who build on. The point of the argument is that the partisans should not hold their leaders in an exalted role but recognize that they are merely servants. The eschatological horizon of 3:10–17 indicates that they are incompetent to judge leaders "before the time" (4:5). Only the day of Christ will reveal the quality of the work. Thus the Corinthians, with standards of judgment that belong to the present age, are incompetent to judge the quality of the ministers before the time.

Paul's discussion discloses his pastoral theology. His pastoral ambition is to ensure that the community survives the ultimate test. The community is now under construction, and the Corinthian partisans are unable to judge the quality of the work. To lay the foundation is only the beginning of the task of building, as Paul's extended metaphor indicates. Ministers are engaged in building a corporate community. To minister is to build on the work of others in the hope of being God's instruments to present the community blameless at the coming of Christ.

15. Richard Hays, "Ecclesiology and Ethics in 1 Corinthians," *Ex auditu* 10 (1994): 37.

Obstacles to Christian Formation in Daily Life (5:1–11:1)

In the new unit that begins in 5:1, Paul turns from the discussion of his role as pastor to address the issues that inhibit the pastoral vision that he enunciates in 1:8. If his goal is a united church on the day of Christ (1:8), the problems mentioned in 5:1–11:1 must be overcome. Here Paul assumes that ministry is the concern for the whole church, for he gives instructions for the conduct of the church in his absence. Paul's pastoral concern for the building of the entire church is the driving force of 5:1–11:1, where he addresses the issues concerning the relationship between the church and the world.[16] The fulfillment of Paul's pastoral vision for a church that is blameless on the day of Christ is now jeopardized by some Corinthians' engagement in practices that undermine the cohesiveness of the community. Entanglements with the old world and insistence on the secular point of view are evident in the Corinthians' insistence on individual rights. The presence of sexual immorality (*porneia*) that would be abhorrent even to Gentiles (5:1) and the litigation among members (6:1–11) before pagan courts destroy the community. The adoption of the phrase "All things are lawful for me" (*panta moi exestin*, 6:12) by the Corinthians reflects their secular understanding of freedom as individual rights. When men interact with the pagan world at banquets at which prostitution is common,[17] they deny their status as a community that has been "washed," "sanctified," and "justified" (6:11).

Paul's primary challenge is to encourage the entire church to accept pastoral responsibility for the continuation of the construction project mentioned in 3:10–17, for only with its involvement in the building of the community will the entire

---

16. See Margaret Mitchell, *Paul and the Rhetoric of Reconciliation* (Louisville: Westminster John Knox, 1991), 225.

17. As already mentioned, Bruce Winter correctly notes that, contrary to the conclusions of most interpreters, Paul does not mention a Corinthian practice of visiting prostitutes. The close connection between the issues in chapters 5–10 indicates that pagan banquets were the occasion for the sexual immorality described in 1 Corinthians. See Winter, *After Paul Left Corinth*, 86–92.

church be blameless on the day of Christ (1:8). Once more he reminds the Corinthians that they stand in the middle of a corporate narrative that began at baptism and will end on the day of Christ. At their baptism, they were incorporated into Israel's narrative (6:11), taking on Israel's mission to be a holy people.[18] Paul therefore encourages them to restore cohesion by "driv[ing] out the wicked person" from their midst (5:13) in the hope that even the sinner will be restored at the day of Christ (5:5). In continuity with Israel, the community metaphorically cleanses itself of all yeast and celebrates the feast, knowing that its paschal lamb has been sacrificed (5:7–8). The community also recognizes that the people of God in the Old Testament are their "ancestors" (10:1) who serve as their examples. Indeed, the fact that those who were once redeemed at the exodus then fell in the wilderness is a reminder to arrogant Corinthians of the consequences of a relapse into idolatry (10:1–13). Paul's warning indicates that the completion of the corporate narrative remains jeopardized unless community members take responsibility for the end of the narrative.

The community's task is to deny the self-serving behavior implied in the slogan *panta moi exestin* in order to become engaged in community construction. Thus Paul corrects the Corinthian slogan and challenges their secular ethics with the corrective "not all things not beneficial" (*ou panta sympherei*, 6:12; 10:23) and "not all things build up" (10:23). Paul insists on an ecclesial ethic—conduct that continues the construction project that he mentions in 3:10–17. Insistence on one's own rights may be a stumbling block (*proskomma*, 8:9) to the one who has a weak conscience and result in the destruction of a "brother for whom Christ died" (8:11; cf. 8:13). If Paul's pastoral vision of a united church on the day of Christ is to be realized, the entire church will recognize that the criterion for Christian behavior is the building of the entire community so that no one is destroyed. Building up (*oikodomē*) is the criterion

18. Hays, "Ecclesiology and Ethics," 39.

for behavior (8:1). Paul wants to see a united church at the parousia, sanctified in Christ. One builds the community only by denying oneself one's own rights. Husbands and wives submit their rights to each other (7:1–4), and members of the community recognize that love "builds up" the community (8:1). Indeed, Paul summarizes his counsel to the Corinthians with the claim "Therefore, if food is a cause of their falling, I will never eat meat, so that I may not cause one of them to fall" (8:13 NRSV). In making himself the model for the behavior that he encourages the Corinthians to adopt, he makes the transition to chapter 9, a digression in the argument that illustrates Paul's own role as an exemplar of self-denying behavior. Paul insists on his apostolic right (*exousia*, 9:12) but insists repeatedly that he did not use his "rights in the gospel" (9:18; cf. 9:15). Indeed, he reaches the climax of his argument in 9:19–23, describing himself as a "slave of all" in order that he might win some. His own ministry is consistent with the pastoral vision of 1:8 insofar as the eschatological vision of a united church determines his ministry. As a model for the Corinthians, he is even weak for the sake of the weak in order that he might win them. Thus he embodies the selfless existence in order to save others.

Just as Paul became subservient to Jews and Greeks (9:19–23), not seeking his own advantage, he concludes this unit with the exhortation to the Corinthians to "give no offense to Jews or Greeks or to the church of God" (10:32). This conduct is an imitation of Paul and an imitation of Christ. Christian formation is therefore to be shaped by the sacrifice of Christ.

Obstacles to Christian Formation in the Assembly (11:2–14:40)

Paul's concern for the cohesion of the church is evident in his response in 11:2–14:40 to the self-serving behavior of the Corinthians in worship. Although we cannot reconstruct the Corinthian situation in detail, we can discern that the Corinthians' individualistic behavior was undermining community solidarity. To some extent, the secular ethics of the Corinthians continued to play a role. Paul indicates that he expects a degree of uniformity in all of his churches (11:16; 14:33).

Paul shapes a community and creates cohesion among all of his churches through traditions that will result in common practice (4:17; 11:2, 16) among churches and shared expectations in local communities. Undoubtedly, in Paul's absence new questions arose about the implementation of the traditions or about their validity, as 11:2–34 indicates. Such issues as different expectations about attire (11:2–16) and social chaos at the Lord's Supper (11:17–34) threaten community solidarity. Although we can only speculate about the issues concerning the roles of men and women in the community, Paul begins and ends this unit with a discussion of their respective roles. His larger concern appears to be the maintenance of common expectations that will be necessary for community life.

Although Paul praises the Corinthians for keeping the traditions in 11:2, he shames the community for its conduct in 11:17–34. When the Corinthians shame those who have nothing, they despise the community of faith. The chaos at the Lord's Supper is an obstacle to Paul's pastoral ambition. Paul restates the community's traditions in 11:23–26 before offering his interpretation in 11:27–34. Here Paul attempts to restore community solidarity between the rich and the poor by placing the whole church before the eschatological judgment of God (11:27–28). Paul's desire for the redemption of the whole community is the basis for his warning about divine judgment. To be guilty of the body and blood is to come under judgment (11:27–31).[19] Recognition of the final judgment is the basis for the instruction to "wait for one another" (11:33). The whole church will stand blameless at the end only if rich and poor can sit at the same table. Paul's pastoral theology requires a

19. Troels Engberg-Pedersen, "Proclaiming the Lord's Death: 1 Corinthians 11:17–34 and the Forms of Paul's Theological Argument," in *Pauline Theology*, ed. Jouette M. Bassler, David M. Hay, and E. Elizabeth Johnson, 4 vols. (Minneapolis: Fortress, 1991–1997), 2:119.

transformation of the secular mind-set of the Corinthians. To participate in the body and blood of Christ is to be conformed to the selflessness demonstrated at the cross.

The Corinthians' self-serving behavior is also evident in the other parts of the assembly, which Paul addresses in chapters 12–14. The Corinthians' overemphasis on glossolalia has apparently resulted in a chaotic assembly. Paul responds to this specific issue, methodically laying the basis in chapter 12 for the specific instructions that he gives in chapter 14. In 12:4–11 he responds to the Corinthians' emphasis on glossolalia by suggesting that each has a gift and that the gifts are intended for "the common good" (12:7). His description of the church as the body of Christ also indicates the solidarity of the community, calling into question the individualism of the Corinthians. This insight is necessary so that there be no division in the body (12:25).

Chapter 12 lays the basis for the specific issue at hand in chapter 14. Over against those who undermine community solidarity, Paul insists that members pursue the gifts that benefit the whole community, not those that involve only the individual and God (14:2). The criterion for worship is to build the whole church (14:4–5). Indeed, Paul insists throughout chapter 14 that *oikodomē* is the norm for the worship of the community. One may notice the repetition of this motif throughout the chapter (14:4–5, 12, 17, 26). Paul expresses concern for the *oikodomē* of the outsiders who come in (14:16). *Oikodomē* requires intelligibility and the willingness to employ one's gifts in an orderly way (14:26). Parallel to *oikodomē* are the other terms for the good of the church (14:3, 6, 19).[20]

As early as 8:1, Paul has demonstrated the close relationship between *agapē* and *oikodomē*. This relationship is further evident in chapter 13, which is a digression in Paul's argument. The celebration of love challenges Corinthian behavior and presents an alternative to their factionalism. According to 13:1–3, love

20. *Paraklēsis* ("encouragement") and *paramythia* ("consolation") appear in 14:3; *ōpheleō* ("benefit") in 14:6; *katēcheō* in 14:19.

is not the alternative to the other gifts but the indispensable quality in the exercise of the gifts. In the description of the attributes of love in 13:4–7, Paul presents the alternative to Corinthian individualism and arrogance. That love is not jealous (13:4) is the alternative to Corinthian conduct. That love is not arrogant is the opposite of Corinthian conduct. In saying that love does not seek its own, Paul reiterates the focus of the preceding arguments. A transformed community will abandon self-seeking for a concern for the other.

The description of the permanence of love in 13:8–13 maintains the eschatological horizon that Paul first introduced in 1:8. At the end of God's grand narrative in which the Corinthians now participate, that is, the day of Christ, only love remains. The community that shares God's narrative will not emphasize gifts that are ultimately transitory, but will devote itself to the gift that remains. As in 3:10–17, Paul emphasizes the certainty of the end, when the transitory will be distinguished from the permanent. He challenges the community to overcome the immaturity of self-seeking and seek the good of others. This love becomes apparent in a community that seeks the *oikodomē* of the church.

The Eschatological Horizon (15:1–58)

The ultimate eschatological horizon is to be seen in the description of the end of the grand narrative in chapter 15. As in earlier parts of the argument (1:8; 3:10–17; 13:8–13), Paul envisions the end (15:24), when the Son delivers all power and authority to the Father. The community of faith that has been transformed into the image of the crucified one (cf. 11:1) will be transformed into the image of Christ, the resurrected one. Those who have been transformed from self-seeking will share in the conclusion to God's narrative. Paul's claim that "we will all be changed" (15:51–53) points to the ultimate description of the destiny of the community. Thus Paul's pastoral theology is determined by the eschatological horizon that he mentions at the beginning (1:8) and end (15:35–58) of the letter. Paul's pastoral ambition will be fulfilled only on the "day of Christ" (1:8) when the community has been transformed. In the meantime the church lives between the beginning and end of its corporate narrative, and its successful completion is threatened. The task of all is to build a community that will survive the test and be blameless at the end. The minister's task is to participate with God in the transformation of the community.

Pastoral Theology in 2 Corinthians

The Pastoral Situation in 2 Corinthians

Despite Paul's victorious statement in 1 Corinthians 15:50–58, when he writes 2 Corinthians the church is no closer to reaching the goal enunciated at the beginning of 1 Corinthians (1:8) inasmuch as the church is scarcely more "blameless" than it was the previous year (cf. 2 Cor. 8:10). The events at Corinth between the two letters have demonstrated how far removed Paul is from the goal of a church that is blameless at the end. Near the beginning of 2 Corinthians Paul describes a disastrous second visit to the Corinthians (2:1–4), and at the end of the letter he expresses the fear of what he will find there on his impending third visit (13:1).

The new situation is the triangular relationship between Paul, the Corinthians, and "some" (or the "many"; cf. 2:17) intruders who commend themselves through letters (cf. 3:1), question Paul's credentials (10:2), and compare themselves to him (10:12). Because Paul's detractors have raised doubts in the minds of the Corinthians about the legitimacy of his ministry, this letter is a defense of Paul's ministry. Although scholars debate whether the letter is a combination of two or more letters, no one doubts that the subject throughout the letter is the same: Paul's defense of his ministry. Unlike other letters of Paul, this letter does not progress toward instructions for conduct in the form of paraenesis. With its focus on the past, it resembles the ancient forensic speech. Like Demosthenes in *Epistulae* 2,

Paul writes to defend his record and his character against the accusations that his opponents have brought against him.[21] The fact that the focus of 2 Corinthians is on Paul's past conduct should not obscure Paul's pastoral vision for the future of the church, as his "anxiety for all the churches" (11:28) defines his ministry. Indeed, Paul's defense of his ministry is intertwined with his emphasis on the ultimate outcome of the construction project that he mentions in 1 Corinthians 3:10–17, for God has appointed him to "build" the community of faith (cf. 2 Cor. 10:8; 12:19; 13:10). This construction project is in jeopardy, as the Corinthians' alienation from Paul is also alienation from God (cf. 5:20–6:2). Therefore, if the major theme of 2 Corinthians is Paul's defense of his ministry, the subordinate theme that is often overlooked is his pastoral vision for the church.

Introducing the Argument: The exordium (1:3–7) and the propositio (1:12–14)

We may observe the relationship between Paul's personal defense and his pastoral ambition for the church in the way that he develops his argument. The opening blessing (1:3–7), with its description of human weakness and divine empowerment, functions as the *exordium*, as it introduces the issues for discussion in a way that is calculated to make the audience favorably disposed. Paul responds to the Corinthians' attack on his weakness with a psalmlike meditation. In the clear statement of the *propositio* of the letter in 1:12–14, Paul summarizes the case that he will develop in the letter. Speaking in the past (aorist) tense, he first indicates that his "boast" is that he has behaved

21. Cf. Frederick Danker, "Paul's Debt to the *De corona* of Demosthenes: A Study of Rhetorical Techniques in Second Corinthians," in *Persuasive Artistry*, ed. Duane F. Watson, Journal for the Study of the New Testament: Supplement Series 50 (Sheffield, Eng.: Sheffield Academic Press, 1991). See also Frances Young and David F. Ford, *Meaning and Truth in 2 Corinthians* (Grand Rapids: Eerdmans, 1988), 27–59; George A. Kennedy, *New Testament Interpretation through Rhetorical Criticism* (Chapel Hill: University of North Carolina Press, 1984), 86.

with sincerity (1:12), anticipating the argument of a letter that consists primarily of Paul's boasting and self-commendation. Indeed, the primary issue of 2 Corinthians is Paul's desire to overcome the suspicions about his ministry. Consequently, the letter is the most autobiographical of Paul's works, as Paul repeatedly commends himself (4:2; 6:4) and "boasts" because he has been forced by his opponents into professional boasting.[22] His boasting becomes especially intense in chapters 10–13, where forms of "boast" (*kauch-*) are used nineteen times.[23] The issue of the entire epistle is Paul's need to respond to those who boast "in outward appearance" (*en prosōpō*, 5:12) and "commend themselves" with others (10:12).

Paul's personal defense cannot be separated from the formation of his churches, as 1:13–14 indicates. He writes not only to justify himself but also to persuade the Corinthians to share his ultimate pastoral vision. He stands in the middle of the community's corporate narrative, hoping that the community will know "until the end" what it already understands "in part": that "on the day of Christ we are your boast even as you are our boast" (1:13–14).[24] This statement recalls Paul's opening prayer in 1 Corinthians that the church be blameless on the day of Christ (1:8) and the prayers in the other letters for the eschatological blamelessness of his churches (Phil. 1:10–11; 1 Thess. 3:11–13). That is, the eschatological horizon determines his ministry. As Paul indicates consistently in the argument of 2 Corinthians, the Corinthians are already his boast and joy. He has great "pride" (*kauchēsis*) and "joy" (*chara*) in the readers (2 Cor. 7:4), and his recent boasting on their behalf has been vindicated by events (7:14). He continues to "boast" of them, anticipating that they will not disappoint him in his

22. Judge, "Paul's Boasting," 46–47.
23. James W. Thompson, "Paul's Argument from Pathos in 2 Corinthians," in *Paul and Pathos*, ed. Thomas Olbricht and Jerry Sumney (Atlanta: Scholars Press, 2001), 134.
24. Note the *inclusio* at the beginning and end of the letter: "I hope you will understand until the end" (1:13). "I hope that you will find out that we have not failed" (13:6).

request for the collection (8:24; 9:1–5). Now he writes to ensure that the Corinthians understand his desire to boast about them at the end. He writes not only to defend his past conduct but to express his concern about the ultimate outcome of the Corinthians. Paul founded this church (cf. 3:3; 11:2), but his work is not complete until the end (cf. 1 Cor. 1:8). The "anxiety for all the churches" (2 Cor. 11:28) defines his ministry.

Paul's pastoral vision in 1:14 corresponds to his consistent description of his pastoral vision of a church that is blameless on the day of Christ (1 Cor. 1:8; Phil. 1:10; 1 Thess. 3:13; cf. Phil. 2:16). Paul envisions the day of Christ when his churches will be fully formed. He knows that his churches will undergo a test before the "day" (1 Cor. 3:13), but he expresses the pastoral goal of the ultimate formation of his churches. He founded the Corinthian church, but his work will not be complete until the day of Christ, when his partnership will be evident in their reciprocal boasting for each other.

The distinctive feature in 2 Corinthians 1:14 is Paul's desire to establish a reciprocity of boasting. He can boast about them only if he is "your boast," for their destinies are intertwined. Paul's self-commendation, defense, and boasting in 2 Corinthians indicate that these goals have not been fulfilled. Although he insists repeatedly that they are his "boast" (cf. 7:2–4, 14), the Corinthians do not boast on his behalf (cf. 12:11; cf. 5:12). Although he boasts of them, he writes under conditions in which they are alienated from him. Therefore he writes to reclaim them and to effect the reciprocity of boasting that he mentions in 1:14. He moves between the past tense (1:15–2:13) and present tense (2:14–7:4), offering his boast in order to reclaim them (5:20–6:2; 6:13; 7:2–4).

Explaining Recent Events (1:15–2:13): The narratio

Paul's unrequited affection for the Corinthians is evident throughout the letter. Despite the community's alienation from him, he indicates his affection for a community more consistently in this letter than in any of the other letters.[25] In his opening benediction (1:3–7) and description of past events (1:8–11; 1:15–2:13), he shows that his ministry is intertwined with theirs as a prelude to the goal expressed in 1:14. His affliction is for their consolation (1:6), and he assumes that they share his sufferings (1:7) and pray on his behalf (1:11). In the narrative of past events (*narratio*) in 1:15–2:13, Paul responds to the suspicions evoked by his change of travel plans, indicating that all of his plans are for their sake (1:23), a demonstration of his love for them (2:4). He responds to open rebellion with forgiveness because it is "for your sake" (2:10). All of his actions have been determined by his desire to fulfill the pastoral goal that he declares in 1:14.

Unrequited Love and a Call for Reciprocity: The probatio (2:14–9:15)

In the main argument (*probatio*) that follows in 2:14–9:15, Paul tries to restore the reciprocity of boasting that is his goal of ministry in 1:14. When he turns to the present tense in 2:14, his personal defense is interwoven with his goal for the formation of the church, for his personal defense is aimed to gain the reciprocity of boasting (cf. 5:12). Paul's defense in 2:14–5:10 prepares the way for the series of appeals to the Corinthians to reciprocate his affection in 5:11–7:16 (cf. 5:20–6:2; 6:11–13; 6:14–7:1; 7:2–3). He speaks in the first person plural in this section, responding to those who doubt his credentials. Against those who criticize his weakness, he describes himself as the captive in a victory processional on his way to death (2:14), distinguishing himself from others who merely peddle the word of God (2:17) and present letters of recommendation (3:1). Paul's letter of recommendation is the community, which he had founded ("ministered by us," 3:3). Just as they are his "boast"

25. R. Bieringer, "Paul's Divine Jealousy: The Apostle and His Communities in Relationship," in *Studies on 2 Corinthians*, ed. R. Bieringer and J. Lambrecht, Bibliotheca ephemeridum theologicarum lovaniensium 112 (Leuven: Leuven University Press, 1994), 248.

(1:14), they are his "letter of recommendation" (3:2). By their continued existence, they "show" (*pheneroumenoi*, 3:3) that they are a letter from Paul and a people empowered by the Spirit (3:6). Not only are they his boast on the day of Christ (1:14); they are his letter of recommendation in the present and the ultimate test of the quality of his ministry.

Paul's echoes of Scripture reveal his pastoral vision. His question in 2:16, "Who is sufficient for these things?" echoes Moses' response to God's call, thus suggesting a comparison between Paul and Moses. His description of himself as "minister of a new covenant" (3:6) indicates his identification with the new covenant of Jeremiah (31:31–34). He is the new Moses, ushering in a new covenant. Thus his people—the Corinthians—are the renewed people of God who have returned from exile. Paul is engaged in the formation of a people through the power of the Spirit (cf. 3:6).

Paul continues to contrast his ministry with that of Moses in 3:7–18, a midrash on the story of Moses' glorious face (Exod. 34:29–35). In 2 Corinthians 3:7–11 Paul does not deny that the ministry of Moses was glorious, but he insists that his ministry of the new covenant is more glorious than that of Moses. In 3:12–18 he contrasts his own boldness with that of Moses, insisting that Moses placed a veil over his face so that the Israelites would not see the end of that which was losing its glory. The contrast is not only between Paul and Moses but between the Israelites, who were unable to see the glory, and the community of faith, made up of those who have turned to the Lord (3:16).

Although Paul's primary focus is the defense of his own ministry, he makes the transition to the inclusion of the church in his reflections of 3:16 and the comment "But when one turns to the Lord, the veil is removed." The church, unlike Israel, has the veil removed. Consequently—Paul moves on to say in 3:18—"we all, with unveiled face . . ." The transition to "we all" includes the community in the story. Unlike the Israelites, who were obscured by a veil, "we all" behold the glory of the Lord with unveiled face. Here is the climax of the discussion.

Paul's destiny is interwoven with that of his church. Those who are the letter written on hearts are the recipients of the Spirit and are being transformed.

One may compare Paul's use of the language of transformation in his letters. In Romans 8:29 the destiny of believers is to be conformed to the image of the son. In Philippians 3:20–21 the Lord will transform the body of lowliness into the body of the glory of Christ. In both cases the ultimate transformation is the day of Christ. In Romans 12:2 Paul speaks in the imperative, "Be transformed by the renewing of your mind." Here, however, Paul speaks in the present passive (*metamorphoumetha*, 2 Cor. 3:18) of a continuing event in which the community joins Paul in taking on the image of Christ. As in Galatians 4:19, Paul assumes a corporate transformation of his community, and his ministry is aimed toward that goal.

The meaning of transformation becomes evident in the continuation of Paul's personal defense in 2 Corinthians 4–7, where he describes his own ministry. According to 4:1–5:10, his life is intertwined with that of the Corinthians. As he preaches that "Jesus Christ is Lord," he is their slave (4:5). Despite his weakness, he does not lose heart (4:1, 16), for his weakness is the occasion for the power of God (4:7). Indeed, as the ultimate sign of weakness, he carries around the dying of Jesus so that the life of Jesus may be manifested in his body (4:10). As one who is "given up [*paradidometha*] to death for Jesus' sake" (4:11), he identifies with the fate of Jesus and takes up the role of the Suffering Servant from Israel's story (Isa. 53:12).[26] The transformation that comes from the Spirit in 2 Corinthians 3:18 is parallel to the power that is present in his weakness. Thus Paul is being transformed into the image of the crucified

26. *Paradidōmi* ("deliver over") is used three times in Isa. 53 for the Suffering Servant (53:6 [twice], 12). In 53:12, the servant "poured out his soul to death" (*paredothē eis thanaton*). Forms of *paradidōmi* taken from Isa. 53:6, 12 are frequently applied to the suffering of Jesus in the New Testament (cf. Matt. 17:22; 20:18–19; Rom. 4:25; 8:32; 1 Cor. 11:23). See William J. Webb, *Returning Home: New Covenant and Second Exodus as the Context for 2 Corinthians 6.14–7.1*, Journal for the Study of the New Testament: Supplement Series 85 (Sheffield, Eng.: JSOT Press, 1993), 104–5.

Christ. In keeping with Paul's focus on reciprocity with his converts, however, he emphasizes his shared narrative with the Corinthians. In saying, "Death is at work in us, but life in you" (4:12), he recalls the Corinthians' share in the partnership. He adds, "because we know that the one who raised the Lord Jesus . . . will bring us with you into his presence" (4:14 NRSV), and, "Everything is for your sake" (4:15), indicating once more his appeal for reciprocity.[27] Thus Paul's ministry is aimed at being joined with the Corinthians at the end (cf. 1:14). He expects the corporate formation of the community.

In his description of his own waiting in 4:16–5:10, Paul's experience of suffering and renewal maintains the eschatological horizon indicated in 1:14. He, with his afflictions, is being renewed every day, analogously to the resurrection power mentioned in 4:7–15. The eschatological horizon stands before him in his suffering and groaning. His experience, however, is also theirs, as "we all" will stand before God (5:10). He anticipates the day when "we all" stand before God. He hopes that they will engage in reciprocal boasting at that time.

That the Corinthians do not reciprocate Paul's pride in them is evident in 5:11–7:16. There he indicates that his defense is intended to bring them to reciprocate his boast on his behalf (5:11–12), and he follows up with a continued defense accompanied by a series of appeals for their reciprocity (cf. 5:20–6:2; 6:11–13; 7:2–4). The pivotal point in Paul's argument is 5:11–6:2, where he restates the letter's thesis statement (1:12–14), indicating that his self-commendation is intended to bring the Corinthians to boast on his behalf (5:11–13). He then offers a theological defense of his ministry (5:14–19) before making the first in a series of appeals to the Corinthians (5:20–6:2).

Paul's claim that his conduct is "for" the Corinthians (5:13) recalls the constant insistence throughout the argument that his love for the community motivates his ministry (cf. 1:23; 2:4). In 5:14–19 he justifies his ministry for others, appealing

---

27. See James W. Thompson, "Reading the Letters as Narrative," in *Narrative Reading, Narrative Preaching*, ed. Joel B. Green and Michael Pasquarello III (Grand Rapids: Baker Academic, 2003), 94.

to the Christian story that "one died for all" as the evidence of the love of Christ that "urges us on." The "for you" quality of his ministry is determined by the fact that "one died for all." Whereas Paul has earlier explained his sacrificial existence in terms of the continuing reality of the cross in his life (1:5; 4:10–15), here his existence for others is based on the death of Jesus as a past event. One may compare his claim in the other letters that he has been "crucified with Christ" (Gal. 2:19) and "become like him in his death" (Phil. 3:10).

In the twofold interpretation of the Christian story in 2 Corinthians 5:14–15, Paul indicates the implications of the Christian narrative for his relationship to the Corinthians. In the first interpretation ("therefore all died"), he includes "all"— the entire believing community—in the Christian narrative. He is linked with the Corinthians as they together share the narrative of Christ. The principle stated in the second interpretation of the Christian story in 5:15 ("that those who live might live no longer for themselves, but for him who died and was raised for them" [NRSV]) applies especially to Paul, but it also links him with every believer who participates in the death of Christ. Just as Paul assumes that "we all" are being transformed into the image of Christ, he assumes that "all" died with Christ and no longer live for themselves. Paul's aim is a transformed community that shares with him the continuing significance of the cross. This outlook includes a totally new epistemology (5:16–17) that is taken up not only by Paul but by "anyone" who is in Christ. This new epistemology, shared by all believers, is the basis for the reciprocity of boasting that Paul desires.

That the Corinthians are not yet transformed is apparent in the appeal of 5:20b–6:2. Paul's appeal to be "reconciled" to God (5:20) indicates that their alienation from him is also alienation from God. In the statement "For our sake he made him to be sin who knew no sin, so that in him we might become the righteousness of God" (5:21 NRSV), Paul repeats the Christian story of the one who died for us, and he indicates the goal of the Christian narrative: "that we might become the righteousness of God in him." This statement is the climax of

Paul's argument. The goal of Christ's death on the cross is not only to save sinners but to transform them and make them the living embodiment of the righteousness of God.[28] Thus the cross is not only an event of the past but the event that continues to transform God's people. In his own suffering, Paul is the embodiment of the transforming effects of the cross. This transformation is not limited to Paul alone, however. The context indicates that "we" refers both to Paul and to his converts, who together "become the righteousness of God." Only then will they engage in the reciprocal boasting at the end that is the goal of his ministry.

Paul's appeals to the Corinthians indicate that this goal remains unfulfilled. His summons not "to receive the grace of God in vain" (6:1) reveals their distance from the destination that Paul envisions. In the remainder of the letter, he describes his pride in the Corinthians and his love for them but concedes that the Corinthians do not return his affection. He concludes his added defense (6:3–10) with an appeal for the Corinthians' response to his affections: "our heart is wide open to you. There is no restriction in our affections, but only in yours. In return—I speak as to children—open wide your hearts also" (6:11–13 NRSV). His appeal for the community to separate from unbelievers (6:14–7:1) belongs to a series of requests for the community's allegiance to Paul.[29] He adds, "Make room for us in your hearts" (7:2), speaking as someone who is under suspicion. Indeed, he indicates his shared destiny with them when he says, "you are in our hearts, to die together and live together" (7:3). This associative language in 7:3 indicates the depth of his relationship to the Corinthians. He indicates his pride in the Corinthians, echoing the thesis statement of the letter (7:4; cf. 1:14), and offers an example when his boasting in the Corinthians was justified (7:5–16). Indeed, recent

28. N. T. Wright, "On Becoming the Righteousness of God," in *Pauline Theology*, ed. Jouette M. Bassler, David M. Hay, and E. Elizabeth Johnson, 4 vols. (Minneapolis: Fortress, 1991–1997), 2:205.
29. See Thompson, "Paul's Argument," 140. See also Webb, *Returning Home*, 31–71.

events have brought joy to Paul, and his boast was not put to shame (7:13–14). Thus the Corinthians, at least in part, have responded appropriately to Paul. Nevertheless, Paul's frequent appeals to the Corinthians indicate that his pastoral goal, enunciated in 1:14, remains in doubt. His boasting on their behalf has not been reciprocated.

In the first seven chapters of 2 Corinthians, Paul has defended himself and indicated that the Corinthians are his "boast," hoping that they will reciprocate. Chapter 7 indicates only that they have responded favorably to the problem of the rebellion of the one who had offended Paul. In the remainder of the letter, Paul turns from the past to the future. In chapters 8 and 9, he continues the theme of his boasting in the Corinthians (8:24; 9:1–5), hoping that they will respond favorably to his boasts. He boasts of the Macedonians, argues that the Corinthians should participate in the collection, and then concludes that their response will be the demonstration of their love and of his boasting on their behalf (8:24). Although he boasts of them to the Macedonians (9:2), he fears that his boasts will be in vain (9:3), inasmuch as the Corinthians have not yet reciprocated Paul's affection for them.

A Final Appeal: The peroratio (10:1–13:14)

In the intensity of the argument in chapters 10–13, Paul reveals the extent of his estrangement from the Corinthians and the remoteness of the pastoral goal that he enunciates in the letter's *propositio* (1:14). With its emotional restatement of the earlier argument, this section is the *peroratio* of the letter. The charges that he must answer (10:10–11; 11:7–11; cf. 12:17–18), the competitive boasting forced upon him by the opponents (10:12–18; 11:12, 18), the bitter irony of the fool's speech (11:16–12:10; cf. 11:19; 12:13), and the Corinthians' willingness to accept the word of the opponents (11:20) indicate the depth of the alienation. The boasting and self-commendation that characterizes this entire section, an elaboration of Paul's initial statement in 1:12, is the result of the Corinthians' failure to boast on Paul's behalf (cf. 12:11). He expresses his fear (cf. 11:3; 12:20) that the Corinthians will abandon their relationship to Christ (11:3) or regress to the immoral way of life they knew before their conversion (12:20–21). Thus Paul's pastoral ambition for the day of Christ, when he and his converts boast of each other, appears to be illusory. Nevertheless, he has not abandoned hope for the ultimate success of his work. His impending visit will be a final attempt to fulfill his pastoral ambition for the Corinthians.

Paul frames the discussion of his pastoral role with the claim that he has the authority "to build and not to tear down" (10:8; 13:10). These words, which are reminiscent of Paul's earlier description of himself as a builder (1 Cor. 3:10), suggest that Paul sees himself in the role of Jeremiah (cf. Jer. 24:6). Although he does "tear down" sophistic arguments (2 Cor. 10:4), his task with the church is to build rather than to tear down. Indeed, he concludes his extensive catalog of sufferings with the affirmation that all of his labors are for the *oikodomē* of the church (12:19). His task as the community's builder is evident in the numerous expressions of affection for the community. He demeans himself by working with his hands, refusing to be a burden, because he wishes to serve them (11:7). When the Corinthians misinterpret his refusal to accept their patronage, he says, "Because I do not love you? God knows I do" (11:11). When he returns for the third visit, he will again refuse to be a burden, for "I do not want what is yours but you" (12:14). Nevertheless, although he is the anxious parent who is ready to "spend and be spent" for them (12:15) and to love them even more, the Corinthians do not reciprocate his affections but respond to his love by questioning his integrity (12:17–18).

Paul's pastoral involvement with his church is nowhere more evident than in his description of himself as the father of the bride who "betrothed you as a pure virgin to Christ" (11:2). The moment of betrothal is the beginning of the church as a corporate community—the equivalent of the task of planting or laying the foundation (1 Cor. 3:5–10). Now he fears that the community's openness to "another Jesus" or "another gospel" (2 Cor. 11:3–4) will preclude his pastoral ambition of presenting the church as a chaste virgin to Christ at the parousia. As he lives between the betrothal and the wedding ceremony, his task of ensuring the fidelity of the bride-to-be is threatened by the forces that have disturbed his work in Corinth.

He concludes the letter with the outcome of the church in doubt. Despite Paul's sacrificial love, the Corinthians have not reciprocated. They desire proof (*dokimē*) that Christ speaks in him (13:3). Just as Paul began the letter with the hope that the Corinthians would understand his ministry (1:13; cf. 5:12), he concludes with the hope that they will understand that he has passed the test (13:6). His ultimate goal, however, is that they do the good even if Paul fails to pass the test (13:7). He rejoices when he is weak but they are strong, and he prays for their *katartisis* (13:9)—the restoration of unity among quarreling parties.[30] In 13:11, using the cognate verb *katartizō*, he encourages them to restore unity among themselves, to agree with one another and to live in peace with one another.[31] Thus we see the entire letter framed by Paul's concern for the outcome of the congregation that he founded. As his "letter of recommendation" and his pride, they determine the significance of his pastoral work.

The Pastoral Implications of the Corinthian Correspondence

For the Corinthian letters, the eschatological vision of a transformed community defines the pastoral task. From the time of the establishment of the church—its planting (1 Cor. 3:5–6), laying of the foundation (3:10), betrothal (11:2)—the cultural forces that undermine this transformation threaten the fulfillment of this goal. The task of ministry is to ensure that the "building," which our predecessors founded and to

30. Bieringer, "Paul's Divine Jealousy," 251.
31. Ibid.

which numerous others have "built on," will survive until the end amid the numerous threats to its existence.

The Corinthians continue to be everywhere, challenging the transforming power of the cross with secular wisdom.[32] Our pastoral ambition is to build the community in the context of the threats posed by the gods of our own age. In the Corinthian correspondence, Paul declares a pastoral theology of transformation that corresponds to the pastoral theology of the other letters. His pastoral theology is ecclesial, cruciform, and eschatological. Although Paul addresses individual issues, his primary task is to ensure that a community composed of individuals from a variety of backgrounds (cf. 1 Cor. 12:12–13) overcomes the barriers of ethnicity and social class to become a demonstration of the unifying power of the cross. Those who abandon self-seeking and unite in a shared narrative of the crucified one will be Paul's boast at the end. The eschatological vision of a blameless community remains the goal of the pastoral ministry. The blameless community has learned the practice of love for others within the community through the cross. Because our work is continually threatened by the cultural forces of individualism, materialism, and ethnic and national pride, the pastoral task remains unfinished. Ministry calls for the continued reminder of the one who did not seek his own.

32. Clyde Fant, *Preaching for Today* (New York: Harper and Row, 1987), 6.

Conclusion

Transformation and Pastoral Theology

As argued in chapter 1, Paul has been the inspiration for numerous attempts to establish a pastoral vision. In the last generation's literature on church growth, Paul's goal is the planting and growing of the church. Traditional attempts to develop a pastoral theology from the Pauline Letters have appealed to two major themes in Romans: justification by faith, and grace as the center of Pauline theology. They have interpreted these categories in individualistic terms, translating them into modern language as the acceptance of the unacceptable. Within this context, the goal of ministry and preaching is to be a channel of grace for the individual. For some, evangelistic preaching has been the channel of grace whereas others have depicted the troubled individual of Romans 7 as the Christian in need of grace mediated through the minister. But the traditional use of Paul for pastoral theology rests on an interpretation that is no longer tenable. Thus, if we are to find insights for ministry from the Pauline correspondence, we must offer an alternative reading of the letters that is based on the use of not only selected passages in 1 Corinthians or Romans but the full range of Paul's correspondence.

The opening chapter argued that we are unable to come to a greater understanding of Paul's view of ministry if we begin with our own definitions of the topic and search for a corollary in the Pauline literature. Rather, we begin with a preliminary definition and then analyze the letters before arriving at a more precise definition of the term (see p. 13). Our reading of the Pauline Letters, with their constant focus on the ethical transformation of communities, leads to a reaffirmation of the definition of ministry offered in the opening chapter: *ministry is participation in God's work of transforming the community of faith until it is "blameless" at the coming of Christ.* This definition assumes a corporate narrative in which the community is unfinished business, standing between its beginning at baptism and its completion at the end. Those who are conformed to the image of the crucified one in selflessness and devotion to others will be transformed into the image of the risen one. The community that has shared the fate of Jesus, dying to its own self-interests, is empowered by God to do God's will. Thus Paul's pastoral ambition, as he states consistently in his letters, is community formation. Although ministry is concerned with the troubled individual, as the contemporary literature on pastoral care makes abundantly clear, the primary focus for Paul's ministry is the formation of communities that will be his boast at the end (Rom. 15:15–16; 2 Cor. 1:12–14; Phil. 2:16; 1 Thess. 2:19).

The consistent theme in all of Paul's letters is a theology of transformation that provides the foundation for his pastoral ambition. Paul's reflections begin with the transformation of Christ, seen in all of the letters. Morna Hooker's description of this transformation as an "interchange" in which Christ "became what we are in order that we might become what he is" provides the basis for Paul's understanding of ministry.[1]

---

1. Morna Hooker, "Interchange in Christ and Ethics," *Journal for the Study of the New Testament* 25 (1985): 5. For a full description of Hooker's idea of "interchange," see ch. 1, above.

Although the language comes from Irenaeus rather than Paul
(*Adversus haereses* 5, praefatio), this feature appears consistently in the letters. Thus the ultimate goal of the minister is to
participate in God's purposes of transformation. Each of the
letters evidences the importance of transformation.

Although the formula of interchange does not appear in
Philippians, this theme is the focus of the letter. At the center of
Philippians is the hymn (Phil. 2:6–11) in which Paul describes
the one who exchanged the *morphē theou* ("form of God") for
the *morphē doulou* ("form of a slave"). He humbled himself
in the most extreme way through death on a cross before God
elevated him to a new status. Paul appeals to the same narrative
in abbreviated form when his appeal to the Corinthians rests
on the fact that "though he was rich, for our sakes he became
poor" (2 Cor. 8:9). In the other letters the narrative consists of
the cross and resurrection. As a shameful means of punishment,
the cross was the ultimate in humiliation. In the resurrection
Paul saw the evidence of the power of God (cf. 2 Cor. 13:4).
Both cross and resurrection—weakness and power—are fundamental for Pauline theology, not only as events of the past
but as facts of abiding significance that cannot be separated
from each other. The resurrected one is also the crucified one,
and the crucified one is also the resurrected one.[2] In the cross
and resurrection, one sees both weakness and power in the
transformation of Jesus Christ.

As a result of the transformation of Christ, believers are
also transformed by participating in the fate of Christ. The
Christian's identity is shaped by the *crucified* Christ, the supreme example of love (Rom. 5:7–8; 2 Cor. 5:14). In the cross of
Christ, "all died," and now they no longer "live for themselves
but for the one who died and arose" (2 Cor. 5:14–15). The
Christian has total identification with the crucified one, and
transformation occurs when the community is shaped by the
sacrifice of the cross. In Philippians the voluntary submission

2. Udo Schnelle, "Transformation und Partizipation in paulinischer Theologie,"
New Testament Studies 47 (2001): 62.

of Christ shapes the mind of believers (Phil. 2:5). In Galatians Paul is the example of one who is "crucified with Christ" (Gal. 2:19), and those who belong to Christ have "crucified the flesh with its desires" (5:24). According to Romans, those who have been baptized participate in the fate of Jesus, dying to an old existence and rising to a new existence (Rom. 6:1–11). As they abandon their old vices, through the power of the Spirit they may now do the good (8:1–13) as they await the ultimate transformation. In 2 Corinthians 8:9, the sacrifice of Christ is the model for the community's generosity. In Romans 15:3 the fact that Christ did not "please himself" becomes the model for community life. The death and resurrection of Christ therefore have a continuing significance for believers, providing them with a totally new identity as a basis for transformation.[3]

Those who are conformed to the death of Christ will ultimately be transformed into the image of the resurrected one. In the meantime, they live out the consequences of the cross, placing the interests of others above their own. Paul consistently elaborates on this theme of transformation, appealing to the story of the crucified one to shape the mentality of the community. Those who adopt this model can "live in harmony with each other" (*to auto phronein*, Phil. 2:2; 4:2). Paul's appeal to the narrative of Christ in Philippians 2:6–11 clearly demonstrates that the community's understanding of love is determined by its adoption of the "mind" (2:5) of the one who exchanged the form of God for the form of a slave. Christian transformation occurs when the community also looks to the interests of others, identifying with the Christ who gave himself for others. Those who identify with the crucified Christ are also empowered by the Christ to be "formed" in the community (Gal. 4:19) as they

3. See Peter Lampe, "Identification with Christ: A Psychological View of Pauline Theology," in *Texts and Contexts*, ed. Tord Fornberg and David Hellholm (Oslo: Scandinavian University Press, 1995), 933–34. According to Lampe (p. 934), the church requires more than other social groups do. The church member not only identifies with the leader but is expected to identify with Christ and to love the other Christians as Christ did. In this way, one goes beyond loving a leader to loving fellow group members.

are incorporated into Christ (3:27–28) and abandon their self-absorption to live for others (5:13–14). To insist on one's own way is not to walk according to love (Rom. 14:15). According to Romans, the ultimate consequence of Paul's doctrine of justification is the creation of a community that transcends ethnic and cultural boundaries and can "live in harmony with one another" (12:16). Its members will not please themselves because Christ did not please himself (15:2–3).

The consistent feature of these letters is the claim that participation in the fate of Christ entails abandoning self-centeredness and progressing in familial love. Paul assumes that believers from different social classes and ethnic groups will be initiated into the community. The test of their progress will be their capacity to exist as family within the community of faith. He offers instructions on the concrete meaning of love, and he assumes that Christian transformation includes continuing progress in learning to live within the family of faith. Those who are shaped accordingly learn to love one another. In Philippians and 1 Thessalonians, we have seen that transformation includes growth in love expressed within the community (Phil. 1:9–11; 1 Thess. 3:11–13). In Galatians and Romans, Paul interprets the love command of Leviticus 19:18 as love within the community of faith.

Because Paul does not separate the weakness of the cross from the power of the resurrection, he insists that God empowers the community to do the will of God. In 1 Thessalonians Paul claims that the word of God empowers the community. In Philippians he says that "God works in you . . . to will and to do" (Phil. 2:13). In both Galatians and Romans, the power of the Spirit enables the community to fulfill the law's requirements. By sharing in the resurrection, its members experience the liberation from sinful passions and the continuing power to do the will of God. In the meantime, God's power is at work in their weakness to ensure their ethical transformation. As they wait for the ultimate righteousness of God (Gal. 5:5), the power of the Spirit enables them to experience ethical transformation. By sharing in the death of Christ, believers abandon the old existence. Because they have entered the new creation (2 Cor. 5:17; Gal. 6:15) and share in the new covenant, they now do the will of God (Jer. 31:31–34; Rom. 8:4). Paul envisions a community that is free from the power of sin.

This understanding of corporate formation is a consistent theme in Paul's letters. In Philippians and 1 Thessalonians, we have seen that the church has a narrative existence. It came into being through the power of God, and it faces a destiny on the day of Christ, when the ultimate transformation will take place. In the meantime Paul expects his churches to make progress toward their final destination by the power of God and the labor of God's ministers. This transformation is evident in the ethical exhortations, which consistently focus on the coming of the kingdom and the return of Christ (cf. Rom. 13:11–14; 1 Cor. 6:9–11; Gal. 5:19).[4] According to 1 Corinthians 3:10–15, the church stands between the laying of the foundation and the final day (3:13), when the quality of the builders' work will become evident. In 2 Corinthians 1:14, Paul anticipates "the day of the Lord Jesus," when he and the congregation will "boast" in each other. Paul is the anxious father of the bride; his aim is to present (*parastēsai*) the church "as a pure virgin to Christ" (2 Cor. 11:2).[5] Ultimately the church will be "conformed to the image of his Son" (Rom. 8:29). Believers who are transformed by the self-emptying of Christ will be transformed (Phil. 3:21) into the image of the glorified son. Thus Paul expects the church to progress toward its goal on the day of Christ, and he assumes that he and other ministers will have a decisive role to play in the transformation of the church.

Paul writes letters to ensure that his churches make progress toward the ultimate goal. In 1 Thessalonians and Philippians,

4. Anton Grabner-Haider, *Paraklese und Eschatologie bei Paulus* (Münster: Aschendorff, 1985), 93.

5. *Parastēsai* involves the presentation of the bride to the bridegroom and the examination of her purity (*hagnotēs*) in association with the wedding (cf. Deut. 22:13; Gen. 29:23). The idea of the return of Christ as the wedding reflects the use of Amos 5:1; Hosea 1–3; Ezek. 16. According to the expectation of Hosea 2:19 and Isa. 62:1–5, God will renew the marriage; Grabner-Haider, *Paraklese*, 93.

we have seen that progress consists of the increasing abundance of the community's love, which is primarily evident in the members' capacity to look to the interests of others within the community. Paul's pastoral task is to ensure this transformation.

The Pauline Model in the Contemporary Church

The historical distance between Paul's communities and the contemporary church prevents us from making the simple transfer of Paul's practice to our own churches. Paul's task was to transform first-generation converts who had made a radical break with their previous existence, whereas our churches belong to a culture that has been influenced by the Christian message. Furthermore, the eschatological urgency that was basic to Paul's theology no longer resonates for us in the same way that it did for Paul. We may note also that life in Paul's house churches was vastly different from that of our affluent and mobile congregations. Nevertheless, we may merge the horizons between Paul's churches and our own and discover in Paul a pastoral theology that is relevant for our own time.[6] The Pauline model would provide a vital reorientation to our own understanding in the following ways.

In the first place, Paul's eschatological orientation provides an alternative view of reality for the foundation for pastoral theology. By initiating his communities into the new creation in anticipation of God's ultimate triumph, he shapes the corporate imagination, creating the potential for the community to see reality in a new way. Ministry becomes not the clarification of the congregation's own values but the transforming of its values through the Christian message. By constantly reaffirming God's grand narrative and the community's place within it, the congregation has the capability of challenging the values of its culture. Paul's view of the final transformation moves the

6. See William Challis, *The Word of Life* (London: Marshall Pickering, 1997), 79; Roland Gebauer, *Paulus als Seelsorger* (Stuttgart: Calwer, 1997), 289.

congregation toward its goal.[7] Under the present circumstances, we always face imperfect churches and individuals. This corporate narrative, however, orients Christian communities to the direction that they will pursue and shapes the task of the pastor and the community.

The eschatological orientation is the foundation for our understanding the goal of both ministry and the church's mission. Paul's affirmation that what matters is neither circumcision nor uncircumcision but a "new creation" (Gal. 6:15) is a reminder that, with the eschatological focus, we can distinguish between the important and the trivial matters. The ultimate test of the effectiveness of our ministry cannot be measured by the standards of our culture or our peers but by whether our work survives the test. With Paul we face the challenge of determining whether our work is "in vain."

In the second place, Pauline pastoral theology challenges the contemporary focus on the individual and emphasizes community formation. The essential characteristic of early spiritual formation is its largely communal character.[8] Although ministry and pastoral care inevitably include engagement with individual struggles, this concern fits within the larger context of the well-being of the entire congregation as it fulfills its mission. The fact that Paul addresses his letters to communities is a reminder that he presupposes the existence of communal memories, conflicts, and challenges. Because this community is based on our shared story rather than the ties of family, ethnicity, or social class, the Pauline model challenges us to build a community that is appropriate to the new creation.

This corporate concern challenges the contemporary focus on self-realization and points to a fulfillment of the self only in relationship to others within the community. The true freedom in Christ is not the satisfaction of our own impulses but the reorientation of the self in community with others who share the common narrative. The church is the place where we un-

7. Stanley P. Saunders, "'Learning Christ': Eschatology and Spiritual Formation in New Testament Christianity," *Interpretation* 56 (2002): 157.
8. Ibid., 158.

derstand that the goal of human life is understood in the light of God's intention for a new humanity.[9] The corporate understanding confronts the balkanizing tendencies in the church, by which we divide into separate interest groups. To build a church on the basis of the satisfaction of consumer tastes is to retreat to the self-centeredness of the old aeon. Furthermore, to divide into "worship wars" determined by the preferences of our own group is to deny the reality of the new community that transcends cultural barriers. The corporate dimension of ministry calls for the building of a community different from what we would have chosen, for we accept those whom God has accepted.

In the third place, ministry will no longer retreat from ethical direction but will offer guidance resulting in ethical transformation. In the new creation, we actually do the will of God by the power of the Spirit. Our shared narrative of the one who gave himself for others creates a new ethical vision in which we do not place our own desires at the center. Paul's focus on two dimensions of the moral life is particularly relevant for our own ministries. His consistent emphasis on a sexual ethic that subordinates the fulfillment of desire to the good of others offers direction to a culture that is dominated by the cult of the self. His focus on love within the community by which we subordinate our own interests to those of others is also ethical direction. Thus he is instrumental in creating a cohesive moral community. The church becomes, as Don Browning says, "a center for moral discourse and decision-making."[10] We meet to reflect on the significance of our shared story for the conduct of our lives.

This ethical transformation means that the task of ministry is not only to communicate God's acceptance of the sinner but also to challenge converts toward transformation. Christ not only died for sinners; he died to reclaim them from the domain of sin. God's grace is renewing, transforming grace as

9. Shirley C. Guthrie Jr., "Pastoral Counseling, Trinitarian Theology, and Christian Anthropology," *Interpretation* 33 (1979): 136.
10. Don S. Browning, *The Moral Context of Pastoral Care* (Philadelphia: Westminster, 1976), 91.

well as forgiving, accepting grace.[11] Although the minister's task is to communicate God's grace and freedom, as the traditional understanding of ministry has held, the minister will also demonstrate that God's grace and freedom calls people to a transformed existence. Evangelism is not mere initiation into a relationship with God but the formation of a community within a narrative that is not yet complete.

Creating the New Congregational Culture

Anyone who has worked in ministry recognizes that the view of ministry offered here is idealistic, and many will consider it totally unrealistic. In our own experience, we have seen only glimpses of this countercultural community that has been described. Unlike Paul, most of us do not plant churches and create their congregational memory. We build on the foundation of others, and our congregations have listened to other voices. We inherit centuries of pastoral ministry that did not envision the task as described here. But I have seen enough glimpses of this new creation in my own experience to be convinced that this Pauline model is viable in the contemporary situation. What I propose has seldom been tried. Our strategies for communal transformation are quite ordinary.

Preaching is the central activity for creating a corporate consciousness. The preacher's concern is not only to engage the listeners in the sermon but to consider the total impact of the ministry of preaching on the communal narrative.[12] Preaching offers a perspective on an alternative world.[13] Paul offers a model of pastoral preaching that shapes the consciousness of the listeners. His constant appeals to the death and resurrection of Christ in the context of the issues confronting his churches indicate that the preaching of the cross opens up this alternative

11. Guthrie, "Pastoral Counseling," 142.
12. See James W. Thompson, *Preaching Like Paul* (Louisville: Westminster John Knox, 2001), 11.
13. Browning, *Moral Context*, 95.

world. The ministry of preaching entails constantly assessing the implications of the cross for shaping our values.

Preaching offers the occasion to explore ethical issues and offer ethical guidelines. In our individualistic culture, we will face resistance. Those of us who want to avoid the older moralism are likely to be reticent to speak in moral terms. We can have a cohesive moral community, however, only when we offer a coherent moral voice on the choices that we face. In Paul we see that the preaching of the cross results in the turning away from self-centeredness to self-denial. In his instructions on sexuality and the passions, Paul attempts to create a countercultural community in which Christians control the passions and live in marital fidelity (cf. 1 Thess. 4:1–7), challenging the dominant ethos of his time. Paul denies that we can do as we please with our own bodies, for we are not our own. We glorify God in our own bodies (1 Cor. 6:20). In our own culture, the Pauline voice continues to offer a countercultural view of sexuality in which we do not seek our own interests but the interests of others.

The alternative vision of the cross also offers an ethical vision of love that extends both to the community of faith and to the larger society. The test of our transformation is the extent to which "the love of Christ controls us" (cf. 2 Cor. 5:14) and results in our care for others within the community. The dominant metaphor for the church in Paul's letters is that of family. He envisions a community in which we care for our aged and disadvantaged, our unemployed and our grief-stricken. To take time for those who are lonely is obviously to take us away from our own pursuits. In an affluent society, we have options for gratifying our own impulses for pleasure, acquisition, or entertainment that tempt us to constant self-absorption. Preaching continues to place before us, however, the alternative vision of an existence for others. If Christians scale back their lifestyles because they learn to identify with the crucified Christ, they will become models for others.[14]

14. Troels Engberg-Pedersen, "Identification with Christ: A Psychological View of Pauline Theology," in *Texts and Contexts*, ed. Tord Fornberg and David Hellholm (Oslo: Scandinavian University Press, 1995), 936.

Within the context of the house church with its limited resources, Paul primarily encouraged his communities to "love one another" within the circle of believers. He gives a glimpse of a love, however, that extends to all (Rom. 12:17; Gal. 6:10). With the resources of our affluent congregations, we have the potential to demonstrate our selfless concern for others in a variety of ways. The use of our time and resources in support of such organizations as Habitat for Humanity, the International Justice Mission, and efforts in our local communities to improve the quality of life for the disadvantaged is evidence of Christian transformation. The sermon is often the one occasion in the church's life when the community gathers to recall its mission and to hear the implications of its story.

Paul's letters remind us that other parts of the liturgy encourage the corporate identity that is necessary for ministry. Inasmuch as the thanksgivings at the beginning of Paul's letters echo the liturgy of his churches, they indicate the importance of corporate prayer in establishing communal identity. Prayers focus congregational consciousness on the community's narrative and establish a vision of God's eschatological goal for the community that prays for transformation and the coming of God's kingdom. Paul's consistent prayer that community members learn to love one another provides a model for corporate prayer within the context of churches that are composed of isolated individuals or subgroups. Prayers of confession may focus not only on private sins but on the weaknesses of a church that continues to "fall short of the glory of God" (Rom. 3:23). Corporate prayer may also focus on the mission of the community as it unites to serve others and proclaim the reign of God.

Paul's instructions in 1 Corinthians 14 remind us that the goal of the entire worship service is to engage in constructing the community (cf. 1 Cor. 14:5). Just as the focal image for ministry is the edification (*oikodomē*) of a community that survives the ultimate test (3:10–17), the test for appropriate worship is the edification (*oikodomē*) of the community. The worship service is not intended to appeal to individual consumer tastes but to build a lasting community. Baptism, the Lord's Supper, and singing celebrate the story that created the community and continues to unite it. Although one may not dismiss the evangelistic dimension of worship or the effect of worship on the outsider, the primary challenge of worship is to contribute to the transformation of the entire community.

If ministry is the transformation of communities into a life shaped by the cross, the church requires models of transformation. In keeping with ancient rhetorical theory, according to which the argument from *ēthos* was an indispensable form of persuasion,[15] Paul regularly appeals to his own transformation and anguish for his communities to show that he participates in both the weakness of the cross and the power of the resurrection (cf. 1 Cor. 4:10–13; 2 Cor. 4:7–16; Gal. 1:10–2:21; Phil. 3:2–21; 1 Thess. 2:1–12). He also points to his coworkers as examples of the transformed existence (cf. Phil. 2:19–30). Paul responds to criticisms of his ministry in Corinth, insisting throughout 2 Corinthians that his ministry is determined by their needs (cf. 2 Cor. 1:23; 4:15). Whereas others think only of themselves, Timothy cares for the Philippians (Phil. 2:20), and Epaphroditus risked his neck for them (2:30). Paul hopes that these models of care for others will shape his own congregations.

This dimension of spiritual formation has been a missing feature in the education of leaders. Because seminary education is rooted in the academic tradition, it focuses on the knowledge and skills that are necessary for managing congregational life. If we consider pastoral care as the formation of communities, the challenge for seminary education is to reconsider how to educate models of Christian transformation.

Ministry is also the task of the entire congregation, as Paul indicates regularly in his letters. This reciprocal ministry has continued relevance in the life of the church today. Although Paul assumes that leaders will take care of pastoral duties (cf.

15. See Thompson, *Preaching Like Paul*, 68.

1 Thess. 5:12), he also assumes that no task is exclusively re-
served for them.[16] Leaders may "admonish" the community
(5:12), but the entire community will "admonish the idlers,
encourage the fainthearted, help the weak" (5:14 NRSV). In
the same way, the entire congregation will encourage the grief-
stricken (4:18). Indeed, Paul frequently uses the metaphor of
the building (*oikodomē*) to describe the role of the entire congregation as it is engaged in the task of constructing an edifice
that survives until the end (cf. 1 Cor. 3:10–17; 8:1, 23; 14:4,
17; 1 Thess. 5:11). As Paul tells the Corinthians in the context
of their corporate worship, believers seek not only to edify
themselves but to edify the entire community (1 Cor. 14:5).
Communal transformation includes the recognition that the
church does not exist to meet our needs but the entire community works to build a lasting structure.

In 2002 I visited a congregation in Ghana where the members are engaged in the building of a school for church leaders. While some of the members have skills in the building
trades to draw the plans and guide the project, other members
of the congregation volunteer their time to make the bricks,
lay the foundation, and build the structure. Since the church
has not borrowed money to construct the building, the project will take many years as the volunteers work together to
complete what the architects have envisioned. The project is
a remarkable example, however, of a congregation where the
individuals place their communal interests above their own in
order to fulfill the church's mission. I am convinced that this
communal culture is a possibility in our own congregations,
not only for literal building projects but also for the building
of the people of God.

The task of ministry is to create the climate in which congregations can be shaped by the cross and pursue the eschatological goal of transformation into the image of the Son. We
meet regularly to reaffirm the story that called us together as

16. See Abraham J. Malherbe, "'Pastoral Care' in the Thessalonian Church," *New
Testament Studies* 36 (1990): 388–89.

a community transcending the barriers of race, gender, and class. Because we have a communal narrative that has not ended, we continue to "increase and abound in love toward one another and for all" (1 Thess. 3:12) as we are transformed by the cross.

Subject Index

Scripture Index

174